A POET'S CHOICE

By Elizabeth Jennings

Elizabeth Jennings

A Poet's Choice

CARCANET

First edition published in 1996 by
Carcanet Press Limited
402-406 Corn Exchange Buildings
Manchester M4 3BY

A CIP catalogue record for this book
is available from the British Library.
ISBN 1 85754 262 2

The publisher acknowledges financial assistance
from the Arts Council of England.

Set in 10 pt Garamond Simoncini by Bryan Williamson, Frome
Printed and bound in England by SRP Ltd, Exeter

For
Blanche, Catherine,
Julia and Katrina

CONTENTS

INTRODUCTION

When I started to assemble this very personal anthology, I knew that it would cover a good deal of ground, but I had no idea how almost immeasurable that ground would be. At the Oxford High School we had, in every class, first-rate teachers of English, and it was there, of course, that my taste began to be formed.

When I was thirteen, and still very much a child, my class was studying certain poems in an anthology called *The Dragon Book of Verse*. One day we read G.K. Chesterton's 'Lepanto'. It was packed with lines like 'Dim drums throbbing in the hills half-heard...', 'The shadow of the Valois is yawning at the Mass', 'Vivat Hispania! Domino gloria! Don John of Austria is riding to the sea.' I was transfigured, totally held; the magic of English verse had taken me over. Miss Thomas, our English mistress and also our form mistress, wrote in the general remarks of that term's school report, 'Latterly she has developed a taste for poetry.' It was much more than that, it was a passion, a total transformation.

We went on to study the romantic poets. I was waiting for the deep excitement 'Lepanto' had given me and I was not disappointed. Keats's odes, Coleridge's *Ancient Mariner* and Shelley's 'Ode to the West Wind' filled me with joy. Of course I did not realise the greatness of these poems but I recognised their power. A term or two later, we were reading a selection of Browning which contained his 'Fra Lippo Lippi' and 'Andrea del Sarto'.

All of this time we had been 'doing' Shakespeare's *Twelfth Night* (far too sophisticated for children), and *Macbeth* (which thrilled me then with its witches). I now find the sheer evil of Macbeth and his wife terrifying. When I was very young I did not think of Shakespeare as poetry.

At the High School we had read Chaucer, Milton, Matthew Arnold and much more. Soon I was doing College Entrance and going up to Oxford. There, C.S. Lewis lectured resonantly on Milton and Courtly Love. Elsewhere Helen Gardner was telling us about Donne.

In the nine papers of our Final Examinations we ended with the death of Shelley. If you were to study the Victorian poets you had to do a tenth paper. Very few candidates did *that*!

I had begun to write pretty terrible verses, though they did use form, when I heard and read 'Lepanto'. At Oxford, some of the lyrics which went into my first book appeared in *Oxford Poetry*, one of whose editors was Kingsley Amis. We became good friends and he introduced me to jazz. Kingsley detested Shakespeare and Milton but did not mind in the least that I enjoyed both.

It has been very difficult to decide what to do about Shakespeare in this anthology. If I had chosen the speeches I enjoy most the book would have overflowed. Instead I decided to give a selection of his sonnets only.

As my choices were beginning to jostle for space I realised that this anthology threatened to flow into two volumes. I have had to cut rigorously and, at times, hurtingly. I decided also to end the book with Wilfred Owen and Edward Thomas. 'Lepanto' had to be included because that poem started this whole happy story.

I have enjoyed much pure pleasure in gathering these poems, and a little prose, together. I am extremely grateful to my publisher for inviting me to make the book. He wanted me to include the poems that had helped to shape my judgement and my art. Many of them are here, along with a few others. I hope that many readers will enjoy *A Poet's Choice* too.

Elizabeth Jennings
August 1996

GEOFFREY CHAUCER

The Prologue

Here biginneth the Book of the Tales of Caunterbury
Whan that Aprille with his shoures sote
The droghte of Marche hath perced to the rote,
And bathed every veyne in swich licour,
Of which vertu engendred is the flour;
Whan Zephirus eek with his swete breeth
Inspired hath in every holt and heeth
The tendre croppes, and the yonge sonne
Hath in the Ram his halfe cours y-ronne,
And smale fowles maken melodye,
That slepen al the night with open yë,
(So priketh hem nature in hir corages):
Than longen folk to goon on pilgrimages
(And palmers for to seken straunge strondes)
To ferne halwes, couthe in sondry londes;
And specially, from every shires ende
Of Engelond, to Caunterbury they wende,
The holy blisful martir for to seke,
That hem hath holpen, whan that they were seke.
  Bifel that, in that seson on a day,
In Southwerk at the Tabard as I lay
Redy to wenden on my pilgrimage
To Caunterbury with ful devout corage,
At night was come in-to that hostelrye
Wel nyne and twenty in a companye,
Of sondry folk, by aventure y-falle
In felawshipe, and pilgrims were they alle,
That toward Caunterbury wolden ryde;
The chambres and the stables weren wyde,
And wel we weren esed atte beste.
And shortly, whan the sonne was to reste,
So hadde I spoken with hem everichon,
That I was of hir felawshipe anon,
And made forward erly for to ryse,
To take our wey, ther as I yow devyse.
  But natheles, whyl I have tyme and space,
Er that I ferther in this tale pace,

1

Me thinketh it acordaunt to resoun,
To telle yow al the condicioun
Of ech of hem, so as it semed me,
And whiche they weren, and of what degree;
And eek in what array that they were inne:
And at a knight than wol I first biginne.

A KNIGHT ther was, and that a worthy man,
That fro the tyme that he first bigan
To ryden out, he loved chivalrye,
Trouthe and honour, fredom and curteisye.
Ful worthy was he in his lordes werre,
And therto hadde he riden (no man ferre)
As wel in Cristendom as hethenesse,
And ever honoured for his worthinesse.

At Alisaundre he was, whan it was wonne;
Ful ofte tyme he hadde the bord bigonne
Aboven alle naciouns in Pruce.
In Lettow hadde he reysed and in Ruce,
No Cristen man so ofte of his degree.
In Gernade at the sege eek hadde he be
Of Algezir, and riden in Belmarye.
At Lyeys was he, and at Satalye,
Whan they were wonne; and in the Grete See
At many a noble aryve hadde he be.
At mortal batailles hadde he been fiftene,
And foughten for our feith at Tramissene
In listes thryes, and ay slayn his fo.
This ilke worthy knight had been also
Somtyme with the lord of Palatye,
Ageyn another hethen in Turkye:
And evermore he hadde a sovereyn prys.
And though that he were worthy, he was wys,
And of his port as meke as is a mayde.
He never yet no vileinye ne sayde
In al his lyf, un-to no maner wight.
He was a varray parfit gentil knight.
But for to tellen yow of his array,
His hors were gode, but he was nat gay.
Of fustian he wered a gipoun
Al bismotered with his habergeoun;
For he was late y-come from his viage,
And wente for to doon his pilgrimage.   ll. 1-78

A YEMAN hadde he, and servaunts namo
At that tyme, for him liste ryde so;
And he was clad in cote and hood of grene;
A sheef of pecok-arwes brighte and kene
Under his belt he bar ful thriftily;
(Wel coude he dresse his takel yemanly:
His arwes drouped noght with fetheres lowe),
And in his hand he bar a mighty bowe.
A not-heed hadde he, with a broun visage.
Of wode-craft wel coude he al the usage.
Upon his arm he bar a gay bracer,
And by his syde a swerd and a bokeler,
And on that other syde a gay daggere,
Harneised wel, and sharp as point of spere;
A Cristofre on his brest of silver shene.
An horn he bar, the bawdrik was of grene;
A forster was he, soothly, as I guesse.

Ther was also a Nonne, a Prioresse,
That of hir smyling was ful and simple and coy:
Hir gretteste ooth was but by sëynt Loy;
And she was cleped madame Eglentyne.
Ful wel she song the service divyne,
Entuned in hir nose ful semely;
And Frensh she spak ful faire and fetisly,
After the scole of Stratford atte Bowe,
For Frensh of Paris was to hir unknowe.
At mete wel y-taught was she with-alle;
She leet no morsel from her lippes falle,
Ne wette hir fingres in hir sauce depe.
Wel coude she carie a morsel, and wel kepe,
That no drope ne fille up-on hir brest.
In curteisye was set ful muche hir lest.
Hir over lippe wyped she so clene,
That in hir coppe was no ferthing sene
Of grece, whan she dronken hadde hir draughte.
Ful semely after hir mete she raughte,
And sikerly she was of greet disport,
And ful plesaunt, and amiable of port,
And peyned hir to countrefete chere
Of court, and been estatlich of manere,
And to ben holden digne of reverence.
But, for to speken of hir conscience,

She was so charitable and so pitous,
She wolde wepe, if that she sawe a mous
Caught in a trappe, if it were deed or bledde.
Of smale houndes had she, that she fedde
With rosted flesh, or milk and wastel-breed.
But sore weep she if oon of hem were deed,
Or if men smoot it with a yerde smerte:
And al was conscience and tendre herte.
Ful semely hir wimpel pinched was;
Hir nose tretys; hir eyen greye as glass;
Hir mouth ful smal, and ther-to softe and reed;
But sikerly she hadde a fair forheed;
It was almost a spanne brood, I trowe;
For, hardily, she was nat undergrowe.
Ful fetis was hir cloke, as I was war.
Of smal coral aboute hir arm she bar
A peire of bedes, gauded al with grene;
And ther-on heng a broche of gold ful shene,
On which ther was first write a crowned A,
And after, *Amor vincit omnia.*   ll. 101-62

　　A MARCHANT was ther with a forked berd,
In mottelee, and hye on horse he sat,
Up-on his heed a Flaundrish bever hat;
His botes clasped faire and fetisly.
His resons he spak ful solempnely,
Souninge alway th'encrees of his winning.
He wolde the see were kept for any thing
Bitwixe Middelburgh and Orewelle.
Wel coude he in eschaunge sheeldes selle.
This worthy man ful wel his wit bisette;
Ther wiste no wight that he was in dette,
So estatly was he of his governaunce,
With his bargaynes, and with his chevisaunce.
For sothe he was a worthy man with-alle,
But sooth to seyn, I noot how men him calle.
　　A CLERK ther was of Oxenford also,
That un-to logik hadde longe y-go.
As lene was his hors as is a rake,
And he nas nat right fat, I undertake;
But loked holwe, and ther-to soberly.
Ful thredbar was his overest courtepy;

4

For he had geten him yet no benefyce,
Ne was so worldly for to have offyce.
For him was lever have at his beddes heed
Twenty bokes, clad in blak or reed,
Of Aristotle and his philosophye,
Than robes riche, or fithele, or gay sautrye.
But al be that he was a philosophre,
Yet hadde he but litel gold in cofre;
But al that he mighte of his freendes hente,
On bokes and on lerninge he it spente,
And bisily gan for the soules preye
Of hem that yaf him wher-with to scoleye.
Of studie took he most cure and most hede.
Noght o word spak he more than was nede.
And that was seyd in forme and reverence,
And short and quik, and ful of hy sentence.
Souninge in moral vertu was his speche,
And gladly wolde he lerne, and gladly teche.
    A SERGEANT OF THE LAWE, war and wys,
That often hadde been at the parvys,
Ther was also, ful riche of excellence.
Discreet he was, and of greet reverence:
He semed swich, his wordes weren so wyse.
Justyce he was ful often in assyse,
By patente, and by pleyn commissioun;
For his science, and for his heigh renoun
Of fees and robes hadde he many oon.
So greet a purchasour was no-wher noon.
Al was fee simple to him in effect,
His purchasing mighte nat been infect.
No-wher so bisy a man as he ther nas,
And yet he semed bisier than he was.
In termes hadde he caas and domes alle,
That from the tyme of king William were falle.
Therto he coude endyte, and make a thing,
Ther coude no wight pinche at his wryting;
And every statut coude he pleyn by rote.
He rood but hoomly in a medlee cote
Girt with a ceint of silk, with barres smale;
Of his array telle I no lenger tale.   ll. 219-330

5

With us ther was a DOCTEUR OF PHISYK,
In al this world ne was ther noon him lyk
To speke of phisik and of surgerye;
For he was grounded in astronomye.
He kepte his pacient a ful greet del
In houres, by his magik naturel.
Wel coude he fortunen the ascendent
Of his images for his pacient.
He knew the cause of everich maladye,
Were it of hoot or cold, or moiste, or drye,
And where engendred, and of what humour;
He was a verrey parfit practisour.
The cause y-knowe, and of his harm the rote,
Anon he yaf the seke man his bote.
Ful redy hadde he his apothecaries,
To sende him drogges and his letuaries,
For ech of hem made other for to winne;
Hir frendschipe nas nat newe to biginne.
Wel knew he th'olde Esculapius,
And Deiscorides, and eek Rufus,
Old Ypocras, Haly, and Galien;
Serapion, Razis, and Avicen;
Averrois, Damascien, and Constantyn;
Bernard, and Gatesden, and Gilbertyn.
Of his diete mesurable was he,
For it was of no superfluitee,
But of greet norissing and digestible.
His studie was but litel on the bible.
In sangwin and in pers he clad was al,
Lyned with taffata and with sendal;
And yet he was but esy of dispence;
He kepte that he wan in pestilence.
For gold in phisik is a cordial,
Therfore he lovede gold in special.
  A good WYF was ther of bisyde BATHE,
But she was som-del deef, and that was scathe.
Of clooth-making she hadde swiche an haunt,
She passed hem of Ypres and of Gaunt.
In al the parisshe wyf ne was ther noon
That to th' offring bifore hir sholde goon;
And if ther dide, certeyn, so wrooth was she,
That she was out of alle charitee.

Hir coverchiefs ful fyne were of ground;
I dorste swere they weyeden ten pound
That on a Sonday were upon hir heed.
Hir hosen weren of fyn scarlet reed,
Ful streite y-teyd, and shoos ful moiste and newe.
Bold was hir face, and fair, and reed of hewe.
She was a worthy womman al hir lyve,
Housbondes at chirche-dore she hadde fyve,
Withouten other companye in youthe;
But therof nedeth nat to speke as nouthe.
And thryes hadde she been at Jerusalem;
She hadde passed many a straunge streem;
At Rome she hadde been, and at Boloigne,
In Galice at seint Jame, and at Coloigne.
She coude muche of wandring by the weye:
Gat-tothed was she, soothly for to seye.
Up-on an amblere esily she sat,
Y-wimpled wel, and on hir heed an hat
As brood as is a bokeler or a targe;
A foot-mantel aboute hir hipes large,
And on hir feet a paire of spores sharpe.
In felawschip wel coude she laughe and carpe.
Of remedyes of love she knew perchaunce,
For she coude of that art the olde daunce.   ll. 411-76

A-morwe, whan that day bigan to springe,
Up roos our host, and was our aller cok,
And gadrede us togidre, alle in a flok,
And forth we riden, a litel more than pas,
Un-to the watering of seint Thomas.
And there our host bigan his hors areste,
And seyde; 'Lordinges, herkneth, if yow leste.
Ye woot your forward, and I it yow recorde.
If even-song and morwe-song acorde,
Lat see now who shal tell the first tale.
As ever mote I drinke wyn or ale,
Who-so be rebel to my jugement
Shal paye for al that by the weye is spent.
Now draweth cut, er that we ferrer twinne;
He which that hath the shortest shal biginne.
Sire knight,' quod he, 'my maister and my lord,
Now draweth cut, for that is myn acord.

7

Cometh neer,' quod he, 'my lady prioresse;
And ye, sir clerk, lat be your shamfastnesse,
Ne studieth noght; ley hond to, every man.'
    Anon to drawen every wight bigan,
And shortly for to tellen, as it was,
Were it by aventure, or sort, or cas,
The sothe is this, the cut fil to the knight,
Of which ful blythe and glad was every wight;
And telle he moste his tale, as was resoun,
By forward and by composicioun,
As ye han herd; what nedeth wordes mo?
And whan this gode man saugh it was so,
As he that wys was and obedient
To kepe his forward by his free assent,
He seyde: 'Sin I shal beginne the game,
What, welcome be the cut, a Goddes name!
Now lat us ryde, and herkneth what I seye.'   ll. 822-55

SIR THOMAS WYATT

'They flee from me'

They flee from me that sometime me did seek
With naked foot stalking in my chamber.
I have seen them gentle, tame, and meek
That now are wild and do not remember
That sometime they put themself in danger
To take bread at my hand, and now they range
Busily seeking with a continual change.

Thanked be fortune it hath been otherwise
Twenty times better, but once in special,
In thin array after a pleasant guise,
When her loose gown from her shoulders did fall
And she caught me in her arms long and small,
Therewithal sweetly did me kiss,
And softly said, 'Dear heart, how like you this?'

It was no dream, I lay broad waking.
But all is turned thorough my gentleness
Into a strange fashion of forsaking;
And I have leave to go of her goodness,
And she also to use newfangleness.
But since that I so kindly am served,
I would fain know what she hath deserved.

EDMUND SPENSER

'Lacking my love'

Lacking my love, I go from place to place,
   Like a young fawn that late hath lost the hind;
   And seek eachwhere, where last I saw her face,
   Whose image yet I carry fresh in mind.
I seek the fields with her late footing signed;
   I seek her bower with her late presence decked;
   Yet nor in field nor bower I her can find,
   Yet field and bower are full of her aspect.
But when mine eyes I thereunto direct,
   They idly back return to me again;
   And when I hope to see their true object,
   I find myself but fed with fancies vain.
Cease then, mine eyes, to seek herself to see;
   And let my thoughts behold herself in me.

SIR PHILIP SIDNEY

'Come sleep'

Come sleep, O sleep, the certain knot of peace,
The baiting place of wit, the balm of woe,
The poor man's wealth, the prisoner's release,
The indifferent judge between the high and low;
    With shield of proof shield me from out the prease
Of those fierce darts despair at me doth throw:
O make in me those civil wars to cease;
I will good tribute pay, if thou do so.
    Take thou of me smooth pillows, sweetest bed,
A chamber deaf to noise, and blind to light;
A rosy garland, and a weary head;
And if these things, as being thine of right,
    Move not thy heavy grace, thou shalt in me,
    Livelier than elsewhere, Stella's image see.

WILLIAM SHAKESPEARE

18

Shall I compare thee to a summer's day?
Thou art more lovely and more temperate.
Rough winds do shake the darling buds of May,
And summer's lease hath all too short a date;
Sometime too hot the eye of heaven shines,
And often is his gold complexion dimm'd,
And every fair from fair sometime declines,
By chance or nature's changing course untrimm'd;
But thy eternal summer shall not fade
Nor lose possession of that fair thou ow'st,
Nor shall death brag thou wander'st in his shade,
When in eternal lines to time thou grow'st.
    So long as men can breathe or eyes can see,
    So long lives this, and this gives life to thee.

29

When, in disgrace with Fortune and men's eyes,
I all alone beweep my outcast state,
And trouble deaf heaven with my bootless cries,
And look upon myself and curse my fate,
Wishing me like to one more rich in hope,
Featur'd like him, like him with friends possess'd,
Desiring this man's art and that man's scope,
With what I most enjoy contented least:
Yet in these thoughts myself almost despising,
Haply I think on thee, and then my state,
Like to the lark at break of day arising,
From sullen earth sings hymns at heaven's gate;
  For thy sweet love remember'd such wealth brings
  That then I scorn to change my state with kings.

42

That thou hast her, it is not all my grief,
And yet it may be said I lov'd her dearly;
That she hath thee is of my wailing chief,
A loss in love that touches me more nearly.
Loving offenders, thus I will excuse ye:
Thou dost love her because thou know'st I love her,
And for my sake even so doth she abuse me,
Suff'ring my friend for my sake to approve her.
If I lose thee, my loss is my love's gain,
And losing her, my friend hath found that loss:
Both find each other, and I lose both twain,
And both for my sake lay on me this cross.
  But here's the joy: my friend and I are one.
  Sweet flattery! Then she loves but me alone.

55

Not marble nor the gilded monuments
Of princes shall outlive this powerful rhyme,
But you shall shine more bright in these contents
Than unswept stone besmear'd with sluttish time.
When wasteful war shall statues overturn
And broils root out the work of masonry,
Nor Mars his sword nor war's quick fire shall burn
The living record of your memory.
'Gainst death and all oblivious enmity
Shall you pace forth; your praise shall still find room
Even in the eyes of all posterity
That wear this world out to the ending doom.
 So, till the judgement that yourself arise,
 You live in this, and dwell in lovers' eyes.

60

Like as the waves make towards the pebbled shore,
So do our minutes hasten to their end;
Each changing place with that which goes before,
In sequent toil all forwards do contend.
Nativity, once in the main of light,
Crawls to maturity, wherewith being crown'd
Crooked eclipses 'gainst his glory fight,
And Time that gave doth now his gift confound.
Time doth transfix the flourish set on youth
And delves the parallels in beauty's brow,
Feeds on the rarities of nature's truth,
And nothing stands but for his scythe to mow.
 And yet to times in hope my verse shall stand,
 Praising my worth despite his cruel hand.

73

That time of year thou mayst in me behold
When yellow leaves, or none, or few, do hang
Upon those boughs which shake against the cold,
Bare ruin'd choirs where late the sweet birds sang.
In me thou seest the twilight of such day
As after sunset fadeth in the west;
Which by and by black night doth take away,
Death's second self, that seals up all in rest.
In me thou seest the glowing of such fire
That on the ashes of his youth doth lie,
As the death-bed whereon it must expire,
Consum'd with that which it was nourish'd by.
 This thou perceiv'st, which makes thy love more strong,
 To love that well which thou must leave ere long.

79

Whilst I alone did call upon thy aid,
My verse alone had all thy gentle grace;
But now my gracious numbers are decay'd,
And my sick Muse doth give another place.
I grant, sweet love, thy lovely argument
Deserves the travail of a worthier pen,
Yet what of thee thy poet doth invent
He robs thee of, and pays it thee again.
He lends thee virtue, and he stole that word
From thy behaviour; beauty doth he give,
And found it in thy cheek: he can afford
No praise to thee but what in thee doth live.
 Then thank him not for that which he doth say,
 Since what he owes thee thou thyself dost pay.

87

Farewell, thou art too dear for my possessing,
And like enough thou know'st thy estimate.
The charter of thy worth gives thee releasing;
My bonds in thee are all determinate.
For how do I hold thee but by thy granting?
And for that riches where is my deserving?
The cause of this fair gift in me is wanting,
And so my patent back again is swerving.
Thyself thou gav'st, thy own worth then not knowing,
Or me to whom thou gav'st it else mistaking;
So thy great gift, upon misprision growing,
Comes home again, on better judgement making.
    Thus have I had thee as a dream doth flatter:
    In sleep a king, but waking no such matter.

88

When thou shalt be dispos'd to set me light
And place my merit in the eye of scorn,
Upon thy side against myself I'll fight,
And prove thee virtuous though thou art forsworn.
With mine own weakness being best acquainted,
Upon thy part I can set down a story
Of faults conceal'd, wherein I am attainted,
That thou in losing me shall win much glory,
And I by this will be a gainer too;
For bending all my loving thoughts on thee,
The injuries that to myself I do,
Doing thee vantage, double-vantage me.
    Such is my love, to thee I so belong,
    That for thy right myself will bear all wrong.

91

Some glory in their birth, some in their skill,
Some in their wealth, some in their body's force,
Some in their garments (though new-fangled ill),
Some in their hawks and hounds, some in their horse;
And every humour hath his adjunct pleasure,
Wherein it finds a joy above the rest.
But these particulars are not my measure;
All these I better in one general best.
Thy love is better than high birth to me,
Richer than wealth, prouder than garments' cost,
Of more delight than hawks or horses be;
And having thee of all men's pride I boast –
    Wretched in this alone, that thou mayst take
    All this away, and me most wretched make.

98

From you have I been absent in the spring
When proud pied April, dress'd in all his trim,
Hath put a spirit of youth in everything,
That heavy Saturn laugh'd and leapt with him.
Yet nor the lays of birds nor the sweet smell
Of different flowers in odour and in hue
Could make me any summer's story tell,
Or from their proud lap pluck them where they grew;
Nor did I wonder at the lily's white,
Nor praise the deep vermilion in the rose.
They were but sweet, but figures of delight
Drawn after you, you pattern of all those;
    Yet seem'd it winter still, and, you away,
    As with your shadow I with these did play.

104

To me, fair friend, you never can be old;
For as you were when first your eye I eyed,
Such seems your beauty still. Three winters cold
Have from the forests shook three summers' pride;
Three beauteous springs to yellow autumn turn'd
In process of the seasons have I seen,
Three April perfumes in three hot Junes burn'd
Since first I saw you fresh, which yet are green.
Ah yet doth beauty like a dial-hand
Steal from his figure, and no pace perceiv'd;
So your sweet hue, which methinks still doth stand,
Hath motion, and mine eye may be deceiv'd.
        For fear of which, hear this, thou age unbred:
        Ere you were born was beauty's summer dead.

109

O never say that I was false of heart,
Though absence seem'd my flame to qualify.
As easy might I from myself depart
As from my soul, which in thy breast doth lie;
That is my home of love. If I have rang'd,
Like him that travels, I return again,
Just to the time, not with the time exchang'd,
So that myself bring water for my stain.
Never believe, though in my nature reign'd
All frailties that besiege all kinds of blood,
That it could so preposterously be stain'd
To leave for nothing all thy sum of good;
        For nothing this wide universe I call,
        Save thou, my rose; in it thou art my all.

116

Let me not to the marriage of true minds
Admit impediments. Love is not love
Which alters when it alteration finds,
Or bends with the remover to remove.
O no, it is an ever-fixed mark
That looks on tempests and is never shaken;
It is the star to every wand'ring bark,
Whose worth's unknown although his height be taken.
Love's not Time's fool, though rosy lips and cheeks
Within his bending sickle's compass come;
Love alters not with his brief hours and weeks,
But bears it out even to the edge of doom.
    If this be error and upon me prov'd,
    I never writ, nor no man ever lov'd.

138

When my love swears that she is made of truth,
I do believe her, though I know she lies,
That she might think me some untutor'd youth
Unlearned in the world's false subtleties.
Thus vainly thinking that she thinks me young,
Although she knows my days are past the best,
Simply I credit her false-speaking tongue;
On both sides thus is simple truth suppress'd.
But wherefore says she not she is unjust?
And wherefore say not that I am old?
O, love's best habit is in seeming trust,
And age in love loves not to have years told.
    Therefore I lie with her, and she with me,
    And in our faults by lies we flatter'd be.

My love is as a fever, longing still
For that which longer nurseth the disease,
Feeding on that which doth preserve the ill,
Th'uncertain sickly appetite to please.
My reason, the physician to my love,
Angry that his prescriptions are not kept,
Hath left me, and I desperate now approve
Desire is death, which physic did except.
Past cure I am, now reason is past care,
And frantic mad with evermore unrest.
My thoughts and my discourse as madmen's are,
At random from the truth, vainly express'd;
    For I have sworn thee fair, and thought thee bright,
    Who art as black as hell, as dark as night.

JOHN DONNE

The Sun Rising

     Busy old fool, unruly Sun,
      Why dost thou thus,
Through windows, and through curtains call on us?
Must to thy motions lovers' seasons run?
     Saucy pedantic wretch, go chide
     Late schoolboys, and sour prentices,
  Go tell Court-huntsmen, that the King will ride,
  Call country ants to harvest offices;
Love, all alike, no season knows, nor clime,
Nor hours, days, months, which are the rags of time.

     Thy beams, so reverend, and strong
      Why shouldst thou think?
I could eclipse and cloud them with a wink,
But that I would not lose her sight so long:
     If her eyes have not blinded thine,

Look, and tomorrow late, tell me,
Whether both th'Indias of spice and mine
Be where thou leftst them, or lie here with me.
Ask for those Kings whom thou sawst yesterday,
And thou shalt hear, All here in one bed lay.

She's all States, and all Princes, I,
Nothing else is.
Princes do but play us; compared to this,
All honour's mimic; all wealth alchemy.
Thou sun art half as happy as we,
In that the world's contracted thus;
Thine age asks ease, and since thy duties be
To warm the world, that's done in warming us.
Shine here to us, and thou art everywhere;
This bed thy centre is, these walls, thy sphere.

A Nocturnal upon S. Lucy's Day
being the shortest day

'Tis the year's midnight, and it is the day's,
Lucy's, who scarce seven hours herself unmasks,
    The Sun is spent, and now his flasks
    Send forth light squibs, no constant rays;
        The world's whole sap is sunk:
The general balm th'hydroptic earth hath drunk,
Whither, as to the bed's-feet, life is shrunk,
Dead and interred; yet all these seem to laugh,
Compar'd with me, who am their Epitaph.

Study me then, you who shall lovers be
At the next world, that is, at the next Spring:
    For I am every dead thing,
    In whom love wrought new alchemy.
        For his art did express
A quintessence even from nothingness,
From dull privations, and lean emptiness:
He ruined me, and I am re-begot
Of absence, darkness, death; things which are not.

All others, from all things, draw all that's good,
Life, soul, form, spirit, whence they being have;
   I, by love's limbeck, am the grave
   Of all, that's nothing. Oft a flood
      Have we two wept, and so
Drowned the whole world, us two; oft did we grow
To be two chaoses, when we did show
Care to aught else; and often absences
Withdrew our souls, and made us carcasses.

But I am by her death (which word wrongs her)
Of the first nothing, the Elixir grown;
   Were I a man, that I were one,
   I needs must know; I should prefer,
      If I were any beast,
Some ends, some means; yea plants, yea stones detest,
And love; all, all some properties invest;
If I an ordinary nothing were,
As shadow, a light, and body must be here.

But I am none; nor will my sun renew.
You lovers, for whose sake, the lesser sun
   At this time to the Goat is run
   To fetch new lust, and give it you,
      Enjoy your summer all;
Since she enjoys her long night's festival,
Let me prepare towards her, and let me call
This hour her vigil, and her Eve, since this
Both the year's, and the day's deep midnight is.

Negative Love

I never stoop'd so low, as they
Which on an eye, cheek, lip, can prey,
   Seldom to them, which soar no higher
   Then virtue or the mind to'admire,
For sense, and understanding may
   Know, what gives fuel to their fire:
My love, though silly, is more brave,

For may I miss, when ere I crave,
If I know yet, what I would have.

If that be simply perfectest
Which can by no way be expressed
   But *Negatives* my love is so.
   To all, which all love, I say no.
If any who deciphers best,
   What we know not, our selves, can know,
Let him teach me that nothing; this
As yet my ease, and comfort is,
Though I speed not, I cannot miss.

The Prohibition

      Take heed of loving me,
At least remember, I forbade it thee;
Not that I shall repair my unthrifty waste
Of Breath and Blood, upon thy sighs and tears,
By being to thee then what to me thou wast;
But, so great Joy, our life at once outwears,
Then, lest thy love, by my death, frustrate be,
If thou love me, take heed of loving me.

      Take heed of hating me,
Or too much triumph in the victory.
Not that I shall be mine own officer,
And hate with hate again retaliate;
But thou wilt lose the style of conqueror,
If I, thy conquest, perish by thy hate.
Then, lest my being nothing lessen thee,
If thou hate me, take heed of hating me.

      Yet, love and hate me too,
So, these extremes shall neither's office do;
Love me, that I may die the gentler way;
Hate me, because thy love's too great for me;
Or let these two, themselves, not me decay;
So shall I live, thy Stage, not triumph be;
Lest thou thy love and hate and me undo,
To let me live, O love and hate me too.

Holy Sonnets

1

Thou hast made me, and shall thy work decay?
Repair me now, for now mine end doth haste,
I run to death, and death meets me as fast,
And all my pleasures are like yesterday;
I dare not move my dim eyes any way,
Despair behind, and death before doth cast
Such terror, and my feeble flesh doth waste
By sin in it, which it towards hell doth weigh;
Only thou art above, and when towards thee
By thy leave I can look, I rise again;
But our old subtle foe so tempteth me,
That not one hour my self I can sustain;
Thy Grace may wing me to prevent his art,
And thou like Adamant draw mine iron heart.

VII

At the round earth's imagin'd corners, blow
Your trumpets, angels, and arise, arise
From death, you numberless infinities
Of souls, and to your scattered bodies go,
All whom the flood did, and fire shall o'erthrow,
All whom war, dearth, age, agues, tyrannies,
Despair, law, chance, hath slain, and you whose eyes
Shall behold God, and never taste death's woe.
But let them sleep, Lord, and me mourn a space,
For, if above all these, my sins abound,
'Tis late to ask abundance of thy grace,
When we are there; here on this lowly ground,
Teach me how to repent; for that's as good
As if thou hadst sealed my pardon with thy blood.

X

Death be not proud, though some have called thee
Mighty and dreadful, for thou art not so,
For those whom thou think'st thou dost overthrow,
Die not, poor death, nor yet canst thou kill me.
From rest and sleep, which but thy pictures be,
Much pleasure, then from thee, much more must flow,
And soonest our best men with thee do go,
Rest of their bones, and soul's delivery.
Thou art slave to fate, chance, kings, and desperate men,
And dost with poison, war, and sickness dwell,
And poppy, or charms can make us sleep as well,
And better than thy stroke; why swell'st thou then?
One short sleep past, we wake eternally,
And death shall be no more; death, thou shalt die.

XVIII

Show me dear Christ, thy spouse, so bright and clear.
What! is it she, which on the other shore
Goes richly painted? or which robbed and tore
Laments and mourns in Germany and here?
Sleeps she a thousand, then peeps up one year?
Is she self truth and errs? now new, now outwore?
Doth she, and did she, and shall she evermore
On one, on seven, or on no hill appear?
Dwells she with us, or like adventuring knights
First travail we to seek and then make Love?
Betray kind husband thy spouse to our sights,
And let mine amorous soul court thy mild Dove,
Who is most true, and pleasing to thee, then
When she is embraced and open to most men.

GEORGE HERBERT

The Agony

      Philosophers have measured mountains,
Fathomed the depths of seas, of states, and kings;
Walked with a staff to heav'n, and tracèd fountains:
      But there are two vast, spacious things,
The which to measure it doth more behove;
Yet few there are that sound them, – Sin and Love.

      Who would know Sin, let him repair
Unto Mount Olivet; there shall he see
A Man so wrung with pains, that all His hair,
      His skin, His garments bloody be.
Sin is that press and vice, which forceth pain
To hunt his cruel food through ev'ry vein.

      Who knows not Love, let him assay
And taste that juice which, on the cross, a pike
Did set again abroach; then let him say
      If ever he did taste the like.
Love is that liquor sweet and most divine,
Which my God feels as blood, but I as wine.

Redemption

Having been tenant long to a rich Lord,
    Not thriving, I resolvèd to be bold,
And make a suit unto Him, to afford
    A new small-rented lease, and cancel th' old.

In heaven at His manor I Him sought:
    They told me there, that He was lately gone
About some land, which he had dearly bought
    Long since on Earth, to take possession.

I straight returned, and knowing His great birth,
  Sought Him accordingly in great resorts –
  In cities, theatres, gardens, parks, and courts:
At length I heard a ragged noise and mirth
  Of thieves and murderers; there I Him espied,
Who straight, 'Your suit is granted,' said, and died.

Easter Wings

Lord, Who createdst man in wealth and store,
    Though foolishly he lost the same,
        Decaying more and more,
            Till he became
                Most poor:
                With Thee
            O let me rise,
        As larks, harmoniously,
    And sing this day Thy victories:
Then shall the fall further the flight in me.

    My tender age in sorrow did begin;
        And still with sicknesses and shame
            Thou didst so punish sin,
                That I became
                    Most thin.
                With Thee
            Let me combine,
        And feel this day Thy victory;
    For, if I imp my wing on Thine,
Affliction shall advance the flight in me.

Prayer

Prayer, the Church's banquet, Angels' age,
    God's breath in man returning to his birth,
The soul in paraphrase, heart in pilgrimage,
    The Christian plummet sounding heav'n and earth;
Engine against th' Almighty, sinner's tower,
    Reversèd thunder, Christ-side-piercing spear,
The six-days-world transposing in an hour,
    A kind of tune which all things hear and fear;
Softness, and peace, and joy, and love, and bliss,
    Exalted manna, gladness of the best,
    Heaven in ordinary, man well dressed,
The milky way, the bird of paradise,
    Church-bells beyond the stars heard, the soul's blood,
    The land of spices, something understood.

The Temper

How should I praise Thee, Lord? how should my rhymes
    Gladly engrave Thy love in steel,
    If, what my soul doth feel sometimes,
        My soul might ever feel!

Although there were some forty heav'ns or more,
    Sometimes I peer above them all;
    Sometimes I hardly reach a score,
        Sometimes to Hell I fall.

O, rack me not to such a vast extent,
    Those distances belong to Thee;
    The world's too little for Thy tent,
        A grave too big for me.

Wilt Thou meet arms with man, that Thou dost stretch
   A crumb of dust from heav'n to hell?
  Will great God measure with a wretch?
    Shall he Thy stature spell?

O, let me, when Thy roof my soul hath hid,
   O, let me roost and nestle there;
  Then of a sinner Thou art rid,
    And I of hope and fear.

Yet take Thy way, for sure Thy way is best:
   Stretch or contract me, Thy poor debter,
  This is but tuning of my breast,
    To make the music better.

Whether I fly with angels, fall with dust,
   Thy hands made both, and I am there;
  Thy power and love, my love and trust,
    Make one place ev'rywhere.

Praise

To write a verse or two is all the praise
    That I can raise:
Mend my estate in any ways,
    Thou shalt have more.

I go to church: help me to wings, and I
    Will thither fly:
Or if I mount unto the sky,
    I will do more.

Man is all weakness; there is no such thing
    As prince or king:
His arm is short; yet with a sling
    He may do more.

A herb distilled and drunk may dwell next door,
                On the same floor,
To a brave soul: exalt the poor,
                They can do more.

O, raise me, then: poor bees, that work all day,
                Sting my delay,
Who have a work as well as they,
                And much, much more.

Affliction

            Kill me not ev'ry day,
Thou Lord of life; since Thy one death for me
        Is more than all my deaths can be,
            Though I in broken pay
Die over each hour of Methusalem's stay.

            If all men's tears were let
Into one common sewer, sea, and brine,
        What were they all compared to Thine?
            Wherein, if they were set,
They would discolour Thy most bloody sweat.

            Thou art my grief alone,
Thou, Lord, conceal it not: and as Thou art
        All my delight, so all my smart:
            Thy cross took up in one,
By way of imprest, all my future moan.

The World

Love built a stately house, where Fortune came;
And spinning fancies, she was heard to say
That her fine cobwebs did support the frame,
Whereas they were supported by the same;
But Wisdom quickly swept them all away.

Then Pleasure came, who, liking not the fashion,
Began to make balcónies, terraces,
Till she had weakened all by alteration;
But reverend laws, and many a proclamation,
Reformèd all at length with menaces.

Then enter'd Sin, and with that sycamore
Whose leaves first sheltered man from drought and dew,
Working and winding slyly evermore,
The inward walls and sommers cleft and tore;
But Grace shored these, and cut that as it grew.

Then Sin combin'd with Death in a firm band
To raze the building to the very floor:
Which they effected, none could them withstand;
But Love and Grace took Glory by the hand,
And built a braver palace then before.

Man

My God, I heard this day
That none doth build a stately habitation
But he that means to dwell therein.
What house more stately hath there been,
Or can be, then is Man? to whose creation
All things are in decay.

For Man is ev'ry thing,
And more: he is a tree, yet bears more fruit;
A beast, yet is, or should be, more:

Reason and speech we only bring;
Parrots may thank us, if they are not mute,
    They go upon the score.

    Man is all symmetry,
Full of proportions, one limb to another,
    And all to all the world besides;
    Each part may call the farthest brother,
For head with foot hath private amity,
    And both with moons and tides.

    Nothing hath got so far
But Man hath caught and kept it as his prey;
    His eyes dismount the highest star;
    He is in little all the sphere;
Herbs gladly cure our flesh, because that they
    Find their acquaintance there.

    For us the winds do blow,
The earth doth rest, heav'n move, and fountains flow;
    Nothing we see but means our good,
    As our delight or as our treasure;
The whole is either our cupboard of food
    Or cabinet of pleasure.

    The stars have us to bed,
Night draws the curtain, which the sun withdraws;
    Music and light attend our head,
    All things unto our flesh are kind
In their descent and being; to our mind
    In their ascent and cause.

    Each thing is full of duty:
Waters united are our navigation;
    Distinguishèd, our habitation;
    Below, our drink; above, our meat;
Both are our cleanliness. Hath one such beauty?
    Then how are all things neat!

    More servants wait on Man
Than he'll take notice of: in ev'ry path
    He treads down that which doth befriend him

When sickness makes him pale and wan.
Oh mighty love! Man is one world, and hath
   Another to attend him.

Since then, my God, Thou hast
So brave a palace built, O dwell in it,
   That it may dwell with Thee at last!
   Till then afford us so much wit,
That, as the world serves us, we may serve Thee,
   And both Thy servants be.

Life

I made a posy while the day ran by:
Here will I smell my remnant out, and tie
   My life within this band;
But Time did beckon to the flowers, and they
By noon most cunningly did steal away,
   And withered in my hand.

My hand was next to them, and then my heart;
I took, without more thinking, in good part
   Time's gentle admonition;
Who did so sweetly Death's sad taste convey,
Making my mind to smell my fatal day,
   Yet sug'ring the suspicion.

Farewell, dear flowers; sweetly your time ye spent,
Fit while ye lived for smell or ornament,
   And after death for cures.
I follow straight, without complaints or grief;
Since if my scent be good, I care not if
   It be as short as yours.

The Collar

I struck the board, and cried, 'No more;
     I will abroad.'
  What, shall I ever sigh and pine?
My lines and life are free; free as the road,
   Loose as the wind, as large as store.
      Shall I be still in suit?
  Have I no harvest but a thorn
  To let me blood, and not restore
What I have lost with cordial fruit?
     Sure there was wine
Before my sighs did dry it; there was corn
   Before my tears did drown it;
  Is the year only lost to me?
   Have I no bays to crown it,
No flowers, no garlands gay? All blasted,
     All wasted?
  Not so, my heart; but there is fruit,
    And thou hast hands.
  Recover all thy sigh-blown age
On double pleasures; leave thy cold dispute
Of what is fit and not; forsake thy cage,
    Thy rope of sands
Which petty thoughts have made; and made to thee
   Good cable, to enforce and draw,
    And be thy law,
  While thou didst wink and wouldst not see.
    Away! take heed;
    I will abroad.
Call in thy death's-head there, tie up thy fears;
    He that forbears
   To suit and serve his need
   Deserves his load,
But as I raved and grew more fierce and wild
    At every word,
  Methought I heard one calling, 'Child';
    And I replied, 'My Lord.'

The Forerunners

The harbingers are come: see, see their mark;
White is their colour, and behold my head.
But must they have my brain? must they dispark
Those sparkling notions which therein were bred?
     Must dullness turn me to a clod?
Yet they have left me, 'Thou art still my God.'

Good men ye be to leave me my best room,
Ev'n all my heart, and what is lodgèd there:
I pass not, I, what of the rest become,
So 'Thou art still my God' be out of fear.
     He will be pleasèd with that ditty;
And if I please Him, I write fine and witty.

Farewell, sweet phrases, lovely metaphors:
But will ye leave me thus? when ye before
Of stews and brothels only knew the doors,
Then did I wash you with my tears, and more,
     Brought you to Church well-drest and clad:
My God must have my best, ev'n all I had.

Lovely enchanting language, sugar-cane,
Honey of roses, whither wilt thou fly?
Hath some fond lover tied thee to thy bane?
And wilt thou leave the Church, and love a sty?
     Fie! thou wilt soil thy broidered coat,
And hurt thyself and him that sings the note.

Let foolish lovers, if they will love dung,
With canvas, not with arras, clothe their shame;
Let Folly speak in her own native tongue:
True Beauty dwells on high; ours is a flame
     But borrowed thence to light us thither:
Beauty and beauteous words should go together.

Yet if you go, I passe not; take your way:
For 'Thou art still my God' is all that ye
Perhaps with more embellishment can say.
Go, birds of Spring; let Winter have his fee;
     Let a bleak paleness chalk the door,
So all within be livelier than before.

SIR THOMAS BROWNE

'The world as text'

Thus, there are two books from whence I collect my divinity: besides that written one of God, another of his servant nature, that universal and public manuscript that lies expansed unto the eyes of all; those that never saw him in the one, have discovered him in the other. This was the scripture and theology of the heathens. The natural motion of the sun made them more admire him than its supernatural station did the children of Israel; the ordinary effects of nature wrought more admiration in them than in the other all his miracles; surely the heathens knew better how to join and read these mystical letters than we Christians, who cast a more careless eye on these common hieroglyphics, and disdain to suck divinity from the flowers of nature. Nor do I so forget God as to adore the name of nature, which I define not with the Schools, the principle of motion and rest, but that straight and regular line, that settled and constant course the wisdom of God hath ordained the actions of his creatures, according to their several kinds. To make a revolution every day is the nature of the sun, because it is that necessary course which God hath ordained it, from which it cannot swerve but by a faculty from that voice which first did give it motion. Now this course of nature God seldom alters or perverts, but like an excellent artist hath so contrived his work that with the selfsame instrument, without a new creation, he may effect his obscurest designs. Thus he sweetened the water with a wood, preserved the creatures in the ark, which the blast of his mouth might have as easily created; for God is like a skilful geometrician, who, when more easily and with one stroke of his compass he might describe or divide a right line, had yet rather do this in a circle or longer way, according to the constituted and forelaid principles of his art; yet this rule of his he doth sometimes pervert, to acquaint the world with his prerogative, lest the arrogancy of our reason should question his power, and conclude he could not; and thus I call the effects of nature the works of God, whose hand and instrument she only is; and therefore to ascribe his actions unto her is to devolve the honour of the principal agent upon the instrument; which if with reason we may do, then let our hammers rise up and boast they have built our houses, and our pens receive the honour of our writings. I hold there is a general beauty in the works of God, and therefore no deformity in any kind or species of creature whatsoever. I cannot tell by what logic we call a toad, a bear, or an elephant ugly, they being created in those outward shapes

34

and figures which best express the actions of their inward forms, and having passed that general visitation of God, who saw that all that he had made was good, that is, conformable to his will, which abhors deformity, and is the rule of order and beauty. There is no deformity but in monstrosity, wherein notwithstanding there is a kind of beauty, nature so ingeniously contriving those irregular parts as they become sometimes more remarkable than the principal fabric. To speak yet more narrowly, there was never anything ugly or misshapen but the Chaos; wherein notwithstanding, to speak strictly, there was no deformity, because no form; nor was it yet impregnate by the voice of God. Now nature is not at variance with art, nor art with nature; they being both the servants of his providence. Art is the perfection of nature. Were the world now as it was the sixth day, there were yet a Chaos. Nature hath made one world, and art another. In brief, all things are artificial, for nature is the art of God.

Religio Medici I.16

'All flesh is grass'

Now for the walls of flesh, wherein the soul doth seem to be immured before the resurrection, it is nothing but an elemental composition, and a fabric that must fall to ashes. 'All flesh is grass' is not only metaphorically, but literally true, for all those creatures we behold are but the herbs of the field, digested into flesh in them, or more remotely carnified in ourselves. Nay, further, we are what we all abhor, anthropophagi and cannibals, devourers not only of men, but of ourselves; and that not in an allegory, but a positive truth; for all this mass of flesh which we behold came in at our mouths; this frame we look upon hath been upon our trenchers. In brief, we have devoured ourselves. I cannot believe the wisdom of Pythagoras did every positively and in a literal sense affirm his metempsychosis, or impossible transmigration of the souls of men into beasts; of all metamorphoses and transformations, I believe only one, that is of Lot's wife, for that of Nebuchadnezzar proceeded not so far. In all others I conceive there is no further verity than is contained in their implicit sense and morality: I believe that the whole frame of a beast doth perish and is left in the same state after death, as before it was materialed unto life; that the souls of men know neither contrary nor corruption, that they subsist beyond the body, and outlive death by the privilege of their proper natures, and without a miracle; that the souls of the faithful as they leave earth take possession of heaven; that those apparitions and ghosts of departed persons are not the wandering souls of men but the unquiet walks of devils, prompting and suggesting us unto mischief, blood, and villainy, instilling and stealing into our hearts that the blessed spirits are not at rest in their graves, but wander solicitous of the affairs of the world. That those phantasms appear often and do frequent cemeteries, charnel houses, and churches, it is because those are the dormitories of the dead, where the devil like an insolent champion beholds with pride the spoils and trophies of his victory in Adam.

Religio Medici I.37

Urn Burial Chapter III

Plastered and whited sepulchres were anciently affected in cadaverous and corruptive burials; and the rigid Jews were wont to garnish the sepulchres of the righteous; Ulysses in *Hecuba* cared not how meanly he lived, so he might find a noble tomb after death. Great persons affected great monuments, and the fair and larger urns contained no vulgar ashes, which makes that disparity in those which time discovereth among us. The present urns were not of one capacity, the largest containing above a gallon, some not much above half that measure; nor all of one figure, wherein there is no strict conformity in the same or different countries, observable from those represented by Casalius, Bosio, and others, though all found in Italy; while many have handles, ears, and long necks, but most imitate a circular figure in a spherical and round composure – whether from any mystery, best duration, or capacity, were but a conjecture. But the common form with necks was a proper figure, making our last bed like our first, nor much unlike the urns of our nativity, while we lay in the nether part of the earth, and inward vault of our microcosm. Many urns are red; these but of a black colour, somewhat smooth, and dully sounding, which begat some doubt whether they were burnt, or only baked in oven or sun, according to the ancient way in many bricks, tiles, pots, and testaceous works, and as the word *testa* is properly to be taken, when occurring without addition; and chiefly intended by Pliny when he commendeth bricks and tiles of two years old, and to make them in the spring. Nor only these concealed pieces, but the open magnificence of antiquity, ran much in the artifice of clay. Hereof the house of Mausolus was built, thus old

Jupiter stood in the Capitol, and the statue of Hercules made in the reign of Tarquinius Priscus was extant in Pliny's days. And such as declined burning or funeral urns, affected coffins of clay, according to the mode of Pythagoras and way preferred by Varro. But the spirit of the great ones was above these circumscriptions, affecting copper, silver, gold, and porphyry urns, wherein Severus lay, after a serious view and sentence on that which should contain him. Some of these urns were thought to have been silvered over, from sparklings in several pots, with small tinsel parcels, uncertain whether from the earth, or the first mixture in them.

Among these urns we could obtain no good account of their coverings; only one seemed arched over with some kind of brickwork. Of those found at Buxton some were covered with flints, some in other parts with tils, those at Yarmouth Caister were closed with Roman bricks; and some have proper earthen covers adapted and fitted to them. But in the Homerical urn of Patroclus, whatever was the solid tegument, we find the immediate covering to be a purple piece of silk; and such as had no covers might have the earth closely pressed into them, after which disposure were probably some of these, wherein we found the bones and ashes half mortared unto the sand and sides of the urn; and some long roots of quitch, or dog's grass, wreathed about the bones.

No lamps, included liquors, lachrymatories, or tear-bottles attended these rural urns, either as sacred unto the *manes*, or passionate expressions of their surviving friends, while with rich flames and hired tears they solemnised their obsequies, and in the most lamented monuments made one part of their inscriptions. Some find sepulchral vessels containing liquors, which time hath incrassated into jellies, for beside these lachrymatories, notable lamps with vessels of oils and aromatical liquors attended noble ossuaries; and some yet retaining a vinosity and spirit in them, which if any have tasted they have far exceeded the palates of antiquity, liquors not to be computed by years of annual magistrates, but by great conjunctions and the fatal periods of kingdoms. The draughts of consulary date were but crude unto these, and Opimian wine but in the must to them.

In sundry graves and sepulchres we meet with rings, coins, and chalices. Ancient frugality was so severe that they allowed no gold to attend the corpse, but only that which served to fasten their teeth. Whether the opaline stone in this urn were burnt upon the finger of the dead, or cast into the fire by some affectionate friend, it will consist with either custom. But other incinerable substances were found so fresh that they could feel no singe from fire. These upon view were judged to be wood, but sinking in water and tried by fire, we found them to be bone or ivory. In their hardness and yellow colour they most resembled box, which in old expressions found the epithet of eternal, and perhaps in such conservatories might have passed uncorrupted. [...]

Gentile inscriptions precisely delivered the extent of men's lives, seldom the manner of their deaths, which history itself so often leaves obscure in the records of memorable persons. There is scarce any philosopher but dies twice or thrice in Laertius, nor almost any life without two or three deaths in Plutarch, which makes the tragical ends of noble persons more favourably resented by compassionate readers, who find some relief in the election of such differences.

The certainty of death is attended with uncertainties in time, manner, places. The variety of monuments hath often obscured true graves, and cenotaphs confounded sepulchres; for beside their real tombs, many have founded honorary and empty sepulchres. The variety of Homer's monuments made him of various countries. Euripides had his tomb in Attica, but his sepulture in Macedonia, and Severus found his real sepulchre in Rome, but his empty grave in Gallia.

He that lay in a golden urn eminently above the earth was not likely to find the quiet of these bones. Many of these urns were broke by a vulgar discoverer in hope of enclosed treasure. The ashes of Marcellus were lost above ground upon the like account. Where profit hath prompted, no age hath wanted such miners: for which the most barbarous expilators found the most civil rhetoric: gold once out of the earth is no more due unto it; what was unreasonably committed to the ground is reasonably resumed from it; let monuments and rich fabrics, not riches, adorn men's ashes; the commerce of the living is not to be transferred unto the dead; it is no injustice to take that which none complains to lose, and no man is wronged where no man is possessor.

What virtue yet sleeps in this *terra damnata* and aged cinders were petty magic to experiment: these crumbling relics and long-fired particles superannuate such expectations. Bones, hairs, nails, and teeth of the dead, were the treasures of old sorcerers. In vain we revive such practices: present superstition too visibly perpetrates the folly of our forefathers, wherein unto old observation this island was so complete that it might have instructed Persia. [...]

He that looks for urns and old sepulchral relics must not seek them in the ruins of temples, where no religion anciently placed them. These were found in a field, according to ancient custom in noble or private burial – the old practice of the Canaanites, the family of Abraham, and the burying place of Joshua, in the borders of his possessions – and also agreeable unto Roman practice to bury by highways, whereby their monuments were under eye, memorials of themselves, and mementoes of mortality unto living passengers, whom the epitaphs of great ones were fain to beg to stay and look upon them, a language sometimes used, not so proper in church inscriptions. The sensible rhetoric of the dead, to exemplarity of good life, first admitted the bones of pious men and martyrs within church walls, which in succeeding ages crept into promiscuous practice; while Constantine was peculiarly favoured to be admitted unto the church porch, and the first thus buried in England was in the days of Cuthred.

Christians dispute how their bodies should lie in the grave. In urnal interment they clearly escaped this controversy. Though we decline the religious consideration, yet in cemeterial and narrower burying places, to avoid confusion and cross position, a certain posture were to be admitted, which even pagan civility observed. The Persians lay north and south, the Megarians and Phoenicians placed their heads to the east, the Athenians, some think, toward the west, which Christians still retain. And Beda will have it to be the posture of our Saviour. That he was crucified with his face towards the west, we will not contend with tradition and public account; but we applaud not the hand of the painter in exalting his cross so high above those on either side, since hereof we find no authentic account in history, and even the crosses found by Helena pretend no such distinction from longitude or dimension. [...]

JOHN MILTON

At a Solemn Music

Blest pair of Sirens, pledges of Heaven's joy,
Sphere-born harmonious Sisters, Voice and Verse,
Wed your divine sounds, and mixed power employ,
Dead things with inbreathed sense able to pierce;
And to our high-raised phantasy present
That undisturbèd Song of pure consent,
Aye sung before the sapphire-coloured Throne

To Him that sits thereon,
With saintly shout and solemn jubily;
Where the bright Seraphim in burning row
Their loud uplifted angel trumpets blow,
And the Cherubic host in thousand quires
Touch their immortal harps of golden wires,
With those just Spirits that wear victorious palms,
Hymns devout and holy psalms
Singing everlastingly:
That we on Earth, with undiscording voice,
May rightly answer that melodious noise;
As once we did, till disproportioned Sin
Jarred against Nature's chime, and with harsh din
Broke the fair music that all creatures made
To their great Lord, whose love their motions swayed
In perfect diapason, whilst they stood
In first obedience, and their state of good.
O, may we soon again renew that song,
And keep in tune with Heaven, till God ere long
To his celestial consort us unite,
To live with Him, and sing in endless morn of light!

L'Allegro

Hence, loathèd Melancholy,
    Of Cerberus and blackest Midnight born,
In Stygian caves forlorn
    'Mongst horrid shapes, and shrieks, and sights unholy,
Find out some uncouth cell,
    Where brooding Darkness spreads his jealous wings,
And the night-raven sings;
    There under ebon shades, and low-browed rocks,
As ragged as thy locks,
    In dark Cimmerian desert ever dwell.
But come, thou Goddess fair and free,
In heaven yclep'd Euphrosyne,
And by men, heart-easing Mirth,
Whom lovely Venus at a birth
With two sister Graces more

To ivy-crownèd Bacchus bore;
Or whether (as some sager sing)
The frolic Wind that breathes the spring,
Zephyr with Aurora playing,
As he met her once a-Maying,
There on beds of violets blue,
And fresh-blown roses washed in dew,
Filled her with thee, a daughter fair,
So buxom, blithe and debonair.

    Haste thee, Nymph, and bring with thee
Jest and youthful Jollity
Quips, and Cranks, and wanton Wiles,
Nods, and Becks, and wreathèd Smiles,
Such as hang on Hebe's cheek,
And love to live in dimple sleek;
Sport that wrinkled Care derides,
And Laughter holding both his sides.
Come, and trip it as ye go,
On the light fantastic toe;
And in thy right hand lead with thee
The mountain Nymph, sweet Liberty;
And, if I give thee honour due,
Mirth, admit me of thy crew,
To live with her, and live with thee,
In unreprovèd pleasures free;
To hear the lark begin his flight,
And singing startle the dull night,
From his watch-tower in the skies,
Till the dappled Dawn doth rise;
Then to come, in spite of sorrow,
And at my window bid good-morrow,
Through the sweet-briar or the vine,
Or the twisted eglantine;
While the cock with lively din
Scatters the rear of Darkness thin;
And to the stack, or the barn-door,
Stoutly struts his dames before:
Oft listening how the hounds and horn
Cheerly rouse the slumbering Morn,
From the side of some hoar hill,
Through the high wood echoing shrill:
Sometime walking, not unseen,

By hedgerow elms, on hillocks green,
Right against the eastern gate,
Where the great Sun begins his state,
Robed in flames and amber light,
The clouds in thousand liveries dight;
While the ploughman, near at hand,
Whistles o'er the furrowed land,
And the milkmaid singeth blithe,
And the mower whets his scythe,
And every shepherd tells his tale
Under the hawthorn in the dale.
    Straight mine eye hath caught new pleasures,
Whilst the lantskip round it measures:
Russet lawns, and fallows gray,
Where the nibbling flocks do stray;
Mountains on whose barren breast
The labouring clouds do often rest;
Meadows trim with daisies pied;
Shallow brooks, and rivers wide.
Towers and battlements it sees
Bosomed high in tufted trees,
Where perhaps some Beauty lies,
The Cynosure of neighbouring eyes.
Hard by, a cottage chimney smokes
From betwixt two aged oaks,
Where Corydon and Thyrsis met
Are at their savoury dinner set
Of hearbs and other country messes,
Which the neat-handed Phillis dresses;
And then in haste her bower she leaves,
With Thestylis to bind the sheaves;
Or, if the earlier season lead,
To the tanned haycock in the mead.
    Sometimes with secure delight
The upland hamlets will invite,
When the merry bells ring round,
And the jocond rebecks sound
To many a youth and many a maid
Dancing in the chequered shade;
And young and old come forth to play
On a sunshine holyday,
Till the livelong daylight fail:

Then to the spicy nut-brown ale,
With stories told of many a feat,
How fairy Mab the junkets eat:
She was pinched and pulled, she said;
And he, by Friar's lanthorn led,
Tells how the drudging Goblin sweat
To earn his cream-bowl duly set,
When in one night, ere glimpse of morn,
His shadowy flail hath threshed the corn
That ten day-labourers could not end;
Then lies him down, the lubber fiend,
And, stretched out all the chimney's length,
Basks at the fire his hairy strength,
And crop-full out of doors he flings,
Ere the first cock his matin rings.
Thus done the tales, to bed they creep,
By whispering winds soon lulled asleep.
Towered cities please us then,
And the busy hum of men,
Where throngs of Knights and Barons bold,
In weeds of peace, high triumphs hold,
With store of Ladies, whose bright eyes
Rain influence, and judge the prize
Of wit or arms, while both contend
To win her grace whom all commend.
There let Hymen oft appear
In saffron robe, with taper clear,
And pomp, and feast, and revelry,
With mask and antique pageantry;
Such sights as youthful Poets dream
On summer eves by haunted stream.
Then to the well-trod stage anon,
If Jonson's learned sock be on,
Or sweetest Shakespeare, Fancy's child,
Warble his native wood-notes wild.
And ever, against eating cares,
Lap me in soft Lydian airs,
Married to immortal verse,
Such as the meeting soul may pierce,
In notes with many a winding bout
Of linkèd sweetness long drawn out
With wanton heed and giddy cunning,

The melting voice through mazes running,
Untwisting all the chains that tie
The hidden soul of harmony;
That Orpheus' self may heave his head
From golden slumber on a bed
Of heaped Elysian flowers, and hear
Such strains as would have won the ear
Of Pluto to have quite set free
His half-regained Eurydice.
These delights if thou canst give,
Mirth, with thee I mean to live.

Lycidas

In this Monody the Author bewails a learned Friend,
unfortunately drowned in his passage from Chester on
the Irish Seas, 1637; and, by occasion, foretells the ruin
of our corrupted Clergy, then in their height.

Yet once more, O ye Laurels, and once more,
Ye Myrtles brown, with ivy never sere,
I come to pluck your berries harsh and crude,
And with forced fingers rude
Shatter your leaves before the mellowing year.
Bitter constraint and sad occasion dear
Compels me to disturb your season due;
For Lycidas is dead, dead ere his prime,
Young Lycidas, and hath not left his peer.
Who would not sing for Lycidas? he knew
Himself to sing, and build the lofty rhyme.
He must not float upon his watery bier
Unwept, and welter to the parching wind,
Without the meed of some melodious tear.
    Begin, then, Sisters of the sacred well
That from beneath the seat of Jove doth spring;
Begin, and somewhat loudly sweep the string.
Hence with denial vain and coy excuse:
So may some gentle Muse
With lucky words favour *my* destined urn,

And as he passes turn,
And bid fair peace be to my sable shroud!

   For we were nursed upon the self-same hill,
Fed the same flock, by fountain, shade, and rill;
Together both, ere the high lawns appeared
Under the opening eyelids of the Morn,
We drove a-field, and both together heard
What time the grey-fly winds her sultry horn,
Battening our flocks with the fresh dews of night,
Oft till the star that rose at evening bright
Toward heaven's descent had sloped his westering wheel.
Meanwhile the rural ditties were not mute;
Tempered to the oaten flute
Rough Satyrs danced, and Fauns with cloven heel
From the glad sound would not be absent long;
And old Damœtas loved to hear our song.

   But, oh! the heavy change, now thou art gone,
Now thou art gone and never must return!
Thee, Shepherd, thee the woods and desert caves,
With wild thyme and the gadding vine o'ergrown,
And all their echoes, mourn.
The willows, and the hazel copses green,
Shall now no more be seen
Fanning their joyous leaves to thy soft lays.
As killing as the canker to the rose,
Or taint-worm to the weanling herds that graze,
Or frost to flowers, that their gay wardrobe wear,
When first the white-thorn blows;
Such, Lycidas, thy loss to shepherd's ear.

   Where were ye, Nymphs, when the remorseless deep
Closed o'er the head of your loved Lycidas?
For neither were ye playing on the steep
Where your old Bards, the famous Druids, lie,
Nor on the shaggy top of Mona high,
Nor yet where Deva spreads her wisard stream.
Ay me! I fondly dream.
'Had ye been there,'...for what could that have done?
What could the Muse herself that Orpheus bore,
The Muse herself, for her inchanting son,
Whom universal nature did lament,
When, by the rout that made the hideous roar,
His gory visage down the stream was sent,

Down the swift Hebrus to the Lesbian shore?
    Alas! what boots it with uncessant care
To tend the homely, slighted, Shepherd's trade,
And strictly meditate the thankless Muse?
Were it not better done, as others use,
To sport with Amaryllis in the shade,
Or with the tangles of Neæra's hair?
Fame is the spur that the clear spirit doth raise
(That last infirmity of noble mind)
To scorn delights and live laborious days;
But the fair guerdon when we hope to find,
And think to burst out into sudden blaze,
Comes the blind Fury with the abhorrèd shears,
And slits the thin-spun life. 'But not the praise,'
Phœbus replied, and touched my trembling ears:
'Fame is no plant that grows on mortal soil,
Nor in the glistering foil
Set off to the world, nor in broad rumour lies,
But lives and spreads aloft by those pure eyes
And perfect witness of all-judging Jove;
As he pronounces lastly on each deed,
Of so much fame in heaven expect thy meed.'
    O fountain Arethuse, and thou honoured flood,
Smooth-sliding Mincius, crowned with vocal reeds,
That strain I heard was of a higher mood.
But now my oat proceeds,
And listens to the Herald of the Sea,
That came in Neptune's plea.
He asked the waves, and asked the felon winds,
What hard mishap hath doomed this gentle swain?
And questioned every gust of rugged wings
That blows from off each beakèd promontory.
They knew not of his story;
And sage Hippotades their answer brings,
That not a blast was from his dungeon strayed:
The air was calm, and on the level brine
Sleek Panope with all her sisters played.
It was that fatal and perfidious bark,
Built in the eclipse, and rigged with curses dark,
That sunk so low that sacred head of thine.
    Next Camus, reverend Sire, went footing slow,
His mantle hairy, and his bonnet sedge,

Inwrought with figures dim, and on the edge
Like to that sanguine flower inscribed with woe.
'Ah! who hath reft,' quoth he, 'my dearest pledge?'
Last came, and last did go,
The pilot of the Galilean Lake;
Two massy keys he bore of metals twain
(The golden opes, the iron shuts amain).
He shook his mitred locks, and stern bespake: –
'How well could I have spared for thee, young swain,
Anow of such as, for their bellies' sake,
Creep, and intrude, and climb into the fold!
Of other care they little reckoning make
Than how to scramble at the shearers' feast,
And shove away the worthy bidden guest.
Blind mouths! that scarce themselves know how to hold
A sheep-hook, or have learnt aught else the least
That to the faithful Herdman's art belongs!
What recks it them? What need they? They are sped;
And, when they list, their lean and fleshy songs
Grate on their scrannel pipes of wretched straw;
The hungry sheep look up, and are not fed,
But, swoln with wind and the rank mist they draw,
Rot inwardly, and foul contagion spread;
Besides what the grim Wolf with privy paw
Daily devours apace, and nothing said.
But that two-handed engine at the door
Stands ready to smite once, and smite no more.'
    Return, Alpheus; the dread voice is past
That shrunk thy streams; return, Sicilian Muse,
And call the vales, and bid them hither cast
Their bells and flowerets of a thousand hues.
Ye valleys low, where the mild whispers use
Of shades, and wanton winds, and gushing brooks,
On whose fresh lap the swart star sparely looks,
Throw hither all your quaint enamelled eyes,
That on the green turf suck the honeyed showers,
And purple all the ground with vernal flowers.
Bring the rathe primrose that forsaken dies,
The tufted crow-toe, and pale gessamine,
The white pink, and the pansy freaked with jet,
The glowing violet,
The musk-rose, and the well-attired woodbine,

With cowslips wan that hang the pensive head,
And every flower that sad embroidery wears;
Bid amaranthus all his beauty shed,
And daffadillies fill their cups with tears,
To strew the laureate hearse where Lycid lies.
For so, to interpose a little ease,
Let our frail thoughts dally with false surmise.
Ay me! whilst thee the shores and sounding seas
Wash far away, where'er thy bones are hurled;
Whether beyond the stormy Hebrides,
Where thou perhaps under the whelming tide
Visit'st the bottom of the monstrous world;
Or whether thou, to our moist vows denied,
Sleep'st by the fable of Bellerus old,
Where the great Vision of the guarded mount
Looks toward Namancos and Bayona's hold.
Look homeward, Angel now, and melt with ruth:
And, O ye dolphins, waft the hapless youth.
     Weep no more, woeful shepherds, weep no more,
For Lycidas, your sorrow, is not dead,
Sunk though he be beneath the watery floor.
So sinks the day-star in the ocean bed,
And yet anon repairs his drooping head,
And tricks his beams, and with new-spangled ore
Flames in the forehead of the morning sky:
So Lycidas sunk low, but mounted high,
Through the dear might of Him that walked the waves,
Where, other groves and other streams along,
With nectar pure his oozy locks he laves,
And hears the unexpressive nuptial song,
In the blest kingdoms meek of joy and love.
There entertain him all the Saints above,
In solemn troops, and sweet societies,
That sing, and singing in their glory move,
And wipe the tears for ever from his eyes.
Now, Lycidas, the Shepherds weep no more;
Henceforth thou art the Genius of the shore,
In thy large recompense, and shalt be good
To all that wander in that perilous flood.

     Thus sang the uncouth Swain to the oaks and rills,
While the still Morn went out with sandals grey:

He touched the tender stops of various quills,
With eager thought warbling his Doric lay:
And now the sun had stretched out all the hills,
And now was dropt into the western bay.
At last he rose, and twitched his mantle blue:
To-morrow to fresh woods, and pastures new.

On His Blindness

When I consider how my light is spent
   Ere half my days in this dark world and wide,
   And that one Talent which is death to hide
   Lodged with me useless, though my soul more bent
To serve therewith my Maker, and present
   My true account, lest He returning chide,
   'Doth God exact day-labour, light denied?'
   I fondly ask. But Patience, to prevent
That murmur, soon replies, 'God doth not need
   Either man's work or his own gifts. Who best
   Bear his mild yoke, they serve him best. His state
Is kingly: thousands at his bidding speed,
   And post o'er land and ocean without rest;
   They also serve who only stand and wait.'

RICHARD CRASHAW

The Hymn of Saint Thomas in Adoration of the Blessed Sacrament

Adoro Te

With all the powers my poor Heart hath
Of humble love and loyal Faith,
Thus low (my hidden life!) I bow to thee
Whom too much love hath bowed more low for me.
Down down, proud sense! Discourses die.
Keep close, my soul's inquiring eye!
Nor touch nor taste must look for more
But each sit still in his own Door.

Your ports are all superfluous here,
Save That which lets in faith, the ear.
Faith is my skill. Faith can believe
As fast as love new laws can give.
Faith is my force. Faith strength affords
To keep pace with those pow'rful words.
And words more sure, more sweet, than they
Love could not think, truth could not say.

O let thy wretch find that relief
Thou didst afford the faithful thief.
Plead for me, love! Allege and show
That faith has farther, here, to go
And less to lean on. Because than
Though hid as GOD, wounds writ thee man,
Thomas might touch; none but might see
At least the suff'ring side of thee;
And that too was thy self which thee did cover,
But here ev'n That 's hid too which hides the other.

Sweet, consider then, that I
Though allowed nor hand nor eye
To reach at thy loved Face; nor can
Taste thee GOD, or touch thee MAN
Both yet believe; and witness thee
My LORD too and my GOD, as loud as He.

Help lord, my Faith, my Hope increase;
And fill my portion in thy peace.
Give love for life; nor let my days
Grow, but in new powers to thy name and praise.

O dear memorial of that Death
Which lives still, and allows us breath!
Rich, royal food! Bountiful BREAD!
Whose use denies us to the dead;
Whose vital gust alone can give
The same leave both to eat and live;
Live ever Bread of loves, and be
My life, my soul, my surer self to me.

O soft self-wounding Pelican!
Whose breast weeps Balm for wounded man.
Ah this way bend thy benign flood
To 'a bleeding Heart that gasps for blood.
That blood, whose least drops sovereign be
To wash my worlds of sins from me.
Come love! Come LORD! and that long day
For which I languish, come away.
When this dry soul those eyes shall see,
And drink the unsealed source of thee.
When Glory's sun faith's shades shall chase,
And for thy veil give me thy FACE.

HENRY VAUGHAN

The Retreat

Happy those early days! when I
Shined in my angel-infancy.
Before I understood this place
Appointed for my second race,
Or taught my soul to fancy ought
But a white, celestial thought,

51

When yet I had not walked above
A mile or two, from my first love,
And looking back (at that short space)
Could see a glimpse of his bright face;
When on some *gilded cloud*, or *flower*
My gazing soul would dwell an hour,
And in those weaker glories spy
Some shadows of eternity;
Before I taught my tongue to wound
My conscience with a sinful sound,
Or had the black art to dispense
A sev'ral sin to ev'ry sense,
But felt through all this fleshly dress
Bright *shoots* of everlastingness.
   O how I long to travel back
And tread again that ancient track!
That I might once more reach that plain,
Where first I left my glorious train,
From whence th' inlightened spirit sees
That shady city of palm trees;
But (ah!) my soul with too much stay
Is drunk, and staggers in the way.
Some men a forward motion love,
But I by backward steps would move,
And when this dust falls to the urn
In that state I came return.

Cheerfulness

Lord, with what courage and delight
        I do each thing
When thy least breath sustains my wing!
        I shine and move
        Like those above,
        And (with much gladness
        Quitting sadness)
Make me fair days of every night.

2

Affliction thus, mete pleasure is,
          And hap what will,
If thou be in't, 'tis welcome still;
          But since thy rays
          In sunny days
          Thou dost thus lend
          And freely spend,
Ah! what shall I return for this?

3

O that I were all Soul! that thou
          Wouldst make each part
Of this poor, sinful frame pure heart!
          Then would I drown
          My single one,
          And to thy praise
          A consort raise
Of *Hallelujahs* here below.

Peace

My soul, there is a country
    Far beyond the stars,
Where stands a wingèd sentry
    All skilful in the wars,
There above noise and danger
    Sweet peace sits crowned with smiles,
And one born in a manger
    Commands the beauteous files,
He is thy gracious friend,
    And (O my soul awake!)
Did in pure love descend
    To die here for thy sake,
If thou canst get but thither,
    There grows the flower of peace,

The Rose that cannot wither,
    Thy fortress and thy ease;
Leave then thy foolish ranges;
    For none can thee secure,
But one, who never changes,
    Thy God, thy life, thy cure.

Corruption

Sure, it was so. Man in those early days
    Was not all stone and earth,
He shined a little, and by those weak rays
    Had some glimpse of his birth.
He saw Heaven o'er his head, and knew from whence
    He came (condemnèd) hither,
And, as first love draws strongest, so from hence
    His mind sure progressed thither.
Things here were strange unto him: sweat and till,
    All was a thorn, or weed,
Nor did those last, but (like himself) died still
    As soon as they did *seed*;
They seemed to quarrel with him; for that Act
    That felled him, foiled them all,
He drew the Curse upon the world, and cracked
    The whole frame with his fall.
This made him long for *home*, as loath to stay
    With murmurers and foes;
He sighed for Eden, and would often say
    Ah! what bright days were those!
Nor was Heav'n cold unto him; for each day
    The valley, or the mountain
Afforded visits, and still Paradise lay
    In some green shade, or fountain.
Angels lay *leiger* here; each bush and cell,
    Each oak and highway knew them,
Walk but the fields, or sit down at some *well*,
    And he was sure to view them.
Almighty *Love*! where art thou now? mad man
    Sits down, and freezeth on,

He raves, and swears to stir nor fire, nor fan,
    But bids the thread be spun.
I see, thy curtains are close-drawn; thy bow
    Looks dim too in the cloud,
Sin triumphs still, and man is sunk below
    The Centre and his shroud;
All's in deep sleep and night; thick darkness lies
    And hatcheth o'er thy people;
But hark! what trumpet's that? what Angel cries
    Arise! Thrust in thy sickle.

The World

I saw Eternity the other night
Like a great *Ring* of pure and endless light,
    All calm, as it was bright,
And round beneath it, Time in hours, days, years
        Driv'n by the spheres
Like a vast shadow moved, in which the world
        And all her train were hurled;
The doting lover in his quaintest strain
        Did there complain,
Near him, his lute, his fancy, and his flights,
        Wit's sour delights,
With gloves and knots, the silly snares of pleasure,
        Yet his dear treasure
All scattered lay, while he his eyes did pore
        Upon a flower.

The darksome statesman hung with weights and woe
Like a thick midnight-fog moved there so slow
    He did not stay, nor go;
Condemning thoughts (like sad eclipses) scowl
        Upon his soul,
And clouds of crying witnesses without
        Pursued him with one shout.
Yet digged the mole, and lest his ways be found
        Worked under ground,

Where he did clutch his prey, but one did see
            That policy,
Churches and altars fed him, perjuries
            Were gnats and flies,
It rained about him blood and tears, but he
            Drank them as free.

The fearful miser on a heap of rust
Sate pining all his life there, did scarce trust
            His own hands with the dust,
Yet would not place one piece above, but lives
            In fear of thieves.
Thousands there were as frantic as himself
            And hugged each one his pelf,
The downright epicure placed heav'n in sense
            And scorned pretence
While others slipped into a wide excess
            Said little less;
The weaker sort slight, trivial wares inslave
            Who think them brave,
And poor, despisèd truth sate counting by
            Their victory.

Yet some, who all this while did weep and sing,
And sing and weep, soared up into the *Ring*,
            But most would use no wing.
O fools (said I) thus to prefer dark night
            Before true light,
To live in grots and caves, and hate the day
            Because it shows the way,
The way which from this dead and dark abode
            Leads up to God,
A way where you might tread the sun, and be
            More bright than he.
But as I did their madness so discuss
            One whispered thus,
This Ring the Bridegroom did for none provide
            But for his bride.

Man

    Weighing the steadfastness and state
Of some mean things which here below reside,
Where birds like watchful clocks the noiseless date
    And intercourse of times divide,
Where bees at night get home and hive, and flowers
        Early, as well as late,
Rise with the sun, and set in the same bowers;

    I would (said I) my God would give
The staidness of these things to man! for these
To his divine appointments ever cleave,
    And no new business breaks their peace;
The birds nor sow, nor reap, yet sup and dine,
        The flowers without clothes live,
Yet Solomon was never dressed so fine.

    Man hath still either toys or care,
He hath no root, nor to one place is tied,
But ever restless and irregular
    About this Earth doth run and ride,
He knows he hath a home, but scarce knows where,
        He says it is so far
That he hath quite forgot how to go there.

    He knocks at all doors, strays and roams,
Nay hath not so much wit as some stones have
Which in the darkest nights point to their homes,
    By some hid sense their Maker gave;
Man is the shuttle, to whose winding quest
        And passage through these looms
God ordered motion, but ordained no rest.

JOHN DRYDEN

A Song for St Cecilia's Day, 1687

1

From harmony, from heav'nly harmony
    This universal frame began.
  When nature underneath a heap
    Of jarring atoms lay,
  And could not heave her head,
The tuneful voice was heard from high,
    'Arise ye more than dead.'
Then cold, and hot, and moist, and dry,
  In order to their stations leap,
    And music's pow'r obey.
From harmony, from heav'nly harmony
    This universal frame began;
    From harmony to harmony
Through all the compass of the notes it ran,
The diapason closing full in man.

2

What passion cannot music raise and quell!
    When Jubal struck the corded shell,
  His list'ning brethren stood around
  And wond'ring on their faces fell
  To worship that celestial sound.
Less than a god they thought there could not dwell
    Within the hollow of that shell,
    That spoke so sweetly and so well.
What passion cannot music raise and quell!

3

The trumpet's loud clangour
    Excites us to arms
With shrill notes of anger
    And mortal alarms.

The double double double beat
   Of the thund'ring drum
   Cries hark the foes come!
Charge, charge, 'tis too late to retreat.

4

The soft complaining flute
In dying notes discovers
The woes of hopeless lovers,
Whose dirge is whisper'd by the warbling lute.

5

Sharp violins proclaim
Their jealous pangs and desperation,
Fury, frantic indignation,
Depth of pains and height of passion,
   For the fair, disdainful dame.

6

But oh! what art can teach
   What human voice can reach
The sacred organ's praise?
Notes inspiring holy love,
Notes that wing their heav'nly ways
    To mend the choirs above.

7

Orpheus could lead the savage race,
And trees uprooted left their place,
   Sequacious of the lyre.
But bright Cecilia raised the wonder high'r;
   When to her organ vocal breath was giv'n,
An angel heard and straight appeared
   Mistaking earth for heav'n.

As from the pow'r of sacred lays
    The spheres began to move,
And sung the great creator's praise
    To all the blessed above;
So when the last and dreadful hour
This crumbling pageant shall devour,
The trumpet shall be heard on high,
The dead shall live, the living die,
And music shall untune the sky.

Alexander's Feast

OR THE POWER OF MUSIC

AN ODE IN HONOUR OF ST CECILIA'S DAY

I

'Twas at the royal feast, for Persia won,
    By Philip's warlike son:
    Aloft in awful state
    The god-like hero sate
    On his imperial throne;
His valiant peers were placed around,
Their brows with roses and with myrtles bound
    (So should desert in arms be crowned).
The lovely Thais by his side
Sate like a blooming Eastern bride
In flow'r of youth and beauty's pride.
    Happy, happy, happy pair!
      None but the brave,
      None but the brave,
    None but the brave deserves the fair.

> Happy, happy, happy pair!
>> None but the brave,
>> None but the brave,
> None but the brave deserves the fair.

II

> Timotheus, placed on high
>> Amid the tuneful quire,
> With flying fingers touched the lyre.
>> The trembling notes ascend the sky,
>> And heav'nly joys inspire.
> The song began from Jove;
> Who left his blissful seats above
> (Such is the pow'r of mighty love).
> A dragon's fiery form belied the god,
> Sublime on radiant spires he rode,
>> When he to fair Olympia press'd;
>> And while he sought her snowy breast,
> Then round her slender waist he curled
And stamped an image of himself, a sov'reign of the world.
> The list'ning crowd admire the lofty sound,
> 'A present deity,' they shout around;
> 'A present deity,' the vaulted roofs rebound.
>>> With ravished ears
>>> The monarch hears,
>>> Assumes the god,
>>> Affects to nod,
> And seems to shake the spheres.

CHORUS

>> With ravished ears
>> The monarch hears,
>> Assumes the god,
>> Affects to nod,
> And seems to shake the spheres.

The praise of Bacchus then the sweet musician sung,
　Of Bacchus ever fair and ever young.
　　The jolly god in triumph comes;
　　Sound the trumpets, beat the drums;
　　　Flushed with a purple grace
　　　He shows his honest face;
Now give the hautboys breath; he comes, he comes.
　　Bacchus ever fair and young,
　　　Drinking joys did first ordain.
　　Bacchus' blessings are a treasure,
　　Drinking is the soldier's pleasure;
　　　Rich the treasure,
　　　Sweet the pleasure;
　　Sweet is pleasure after pain.

CHORUS

　　Bacchus' blessings are a treasure,
　　Drinking is the soldier's pleasure;
　　　Rich the treasure,
　　　Sweet the pleasure;
　　Sweet is pleasure after pain.

IV

　Soothed with the sound the King grew vain;
　　Fought all his battles o'er again;
And thrice he routed all his foes, and thrice he slew the slain.
　　The master saw the madness rise;
　　His glowing cheeks, his ardent eyes;
　　And while he heav'n and earth defied,
　　Changed his hand and checked his pride.
　　　He chose a mournful muse
　　　Soft pity to infuse.
　　He sung Darius, great and good,
　　　By too severe a fate
　　Fallen, fallen, fallen, fallen,
　　　Fallen from his high estate
　　And welt'ring in his blood.

62

Deserted at his utmost need
By those his former bounty fed;
On the bare earth exposed he lies,
With not a friend to close his eyes.
With downcast looks the joyless victor sate,
  Revolving in his altered soul
    The various turns of chance below;
  And now and then a sigh he stole,
    And tears began to flow.

CHORUS

  Revolving in his altered soul
    The various turns of chance below;
  And now and then a sigh he stole,
    And tears began to flow.

V

The mighty master smiled to see
That love was in the next degree;
'Twas but a kindred-sound to move,
For pity melts the mind to love.
  Softly sweet, in Lydian measures,
  Soon he soothed his soul to pleasures.
War, he sung, is toil and trouble;
Honour but an empty bubble.
  Never ending, still beginning,
Fighting still, and still destroying,
  If the world be worth thy winning,
Think, O think, it worth enjoying.
  Lovely Thais sits beside thee;
  Take the good the gods provide thee.

The many rend the skies with loud applause;
So love was crowned, but music won the cause.
  The Prince, unable to conceal his pain,
    Gazed on the fair
    Who caused his care,
  And sighed and looked, sighed and looked,
  Sighed and looked, and sighed again.

At length, with love and wine at once oppressed,
The vanquished victor sunk upon her breast.

The Prince, unable to conceal his pain,
  Gazed on the fair
  Who caused his care,
 And sighed and looked, sighed and looked,
 Sighed and looked, and sighed again.
At length, with love and wine at once oppressed,
The vanquished victor sunk upon her breast.

   VI

Now strike the golden lyre again;
A louder yet and yet a louder strain.
Break his bands of sleep asunder
And rouse him, like a rattling peal of thunder.
 Hark, hark, the horrid sound
  Has raised up his head
  As awaked from the dead,
 And amazed he stares around.
Revenge, revenge, Timotheus cries,
  See the Furies arise!
  See the snakes that they rear,
  How they hiss in their hair,
 And the sparkles that flash from their eyes!
  Behold a ghastly band,
  Each a torch in his hand!
Those are Grecian ghosts that in battle were slain,
  And unburied remain
  Inglorious on the plain.
  Give the vengeance due
  To the valiant crew.
Behold how they toss their torches on high,
 How they point to the Persian abodes,
And glitt'ring temples of their hostile gods!
The princes applaud with a furious joy,
And the King seized a flambeau with zeal to destroy;
  Thais led the way

To light him to his prey
And, like another Helen, fired another Troy.

CHORUS

And the King seized a flambeau with zeal to destroy;
    Thais led the way
    To light him to his prey
And, like another Helen, fired another Troy.

VII

    Thus, long ago,
Ere heaving bellows learned to blow,
    While organs yet were mute;
    Timotheus, to his breathing flute
    And sounding lyre,
Could swell the soul to rage or kindle soft desire.
    At last divine Cecilia came,
    Invent'ress of the vocal frame.
The sweet enthusiast, from her sacred store,
    Enlarged the former narrow bounds,
    And added length to solemn sounds,
With nature's mother-wit and arts unknown before.
    Let old Timotheus yield the prize,
        Or both divide the crown;
    He raised a mortal to the skies;
        She drew an angel down.

GRAND CHORUS

    At last divine Cecilia came,
    Invent'ress of the vocal frame.
The sweet enthusiast, from her sacred store,
    Enlarged the former narrow bounds,
    And added length to solemn sounds,
With nature's mother-wit and arts unknown before.
    Let old Timotheus yield the prize,
        Or both divide the crown;
    He raised a mortal to the skies;
        She drew an angel down.

from *An Essay of Dramatic Poesy*

'The end of tragedies or serious plays, says Aristotle, is to beget admiration, compassion or concernment; but are not mirth and compassion things incompatible? and is it not evident that the poet must of necessity destroy the former by intermingling of the latter? that is, he must ruin the sole end and object of his tragedy to introduce somewhat that is forced into it and is not of the body of it. Would you not think that physician mad who having prescribed a purge should immediately order you to take restringents?

'But to leave our plays and return to theirs: I have noted one great advantage they have had in the plotting of their tragedies; that is they are always grounded upon some known history, according to that of Horace, *Ex noto fictum carmen sequar*,[1] and in that they have so imitated the ancients that they have surpassed them. For the ancients, as was observed before, took for the foundation of their plays some poetical fiction such as under that consideration could move but little concernment in the audience because they already knew the event of it. But the French goes farther:

> *Atque ita mentitur; sic veris falsa remiscet,*
> *Primo ne medium, medio ne discrepet imum.*[2]

He so interweaves truth with probable fiction, that he puts a pleasing fallacy upon us, mends the intrigues of fate and dispenses with the severity of history to reward that virtue which has been rendered to us there unfortunate. Sometimes the story has left the success so doubtful that the writer is free, by the privilege of a poet, to take that which of two or more relations will best suit with his design, as, for example, in the death of Cyrus, whom Justin and some others report to have perished in the Scythian war but Xenophon affirms to have died in his bed of extreme old age. Nay more, when the event is past dispute even then we are willing to be deceived, and the poet, if he contrives it with appearance of truth, has all the audience of his party, at least during the time his play is acting; so naturally we are kind to virtue, when our own interest is not in question, that we take it up as the general concernment of mankind. On the other side, if you consider the historical plays of Shakespeare, they are rather so many chronicles of kings, or the business many times of thirty or forty years, cramped into a representation

---

[1] I should pursue my poetic invention upon a basis of known themes. (*Ars Poetica* 240.)

[2] And thus he spins fictions; so does he mingle the false with the true, that the middle may not clash with the beginning, nor the end with the middle. (*Ars Poetica* 151-2.)

of two hours and a half, which is not to imitate or paint nature but rather to draw her in miniature; to take her in little; to look upon her through the wrong end of a perspective, and receive her images not only much less but infinitely more imperfect than the life. This, instead of making a play delightful, renders it ridiculous.

Quodcunque ostendis mihi sic, incredulus odi.[1]

For the spirit of man cannot be satisfied but with truth, or at least veri-simility; and a poem is to contain, if not τὰ ἔτυμα,[2] yet ἐτύμοισιν ὁμοῖα,[3] as one of the Greek poets has expressed it.

'Another thing in which the French differ from us and from the Spaniards is that they do not embarrass or cumber themselves with too much plot; they only represent so much of a story as will constitute one whole and great action sufficient for a play; we, who undertake more, do but multiply adventures: which, not being produced from one another, as effects from causes, but barely following, constitute many actions in the drama, and consequently make it many plays.

'But by pursuing closely one argument, which is not cloyed with many turns, the French have gained more liberty for verse, in which they write; they have leisure to dwell on a subject which deserves it; and to represent the passions (which we have acknowledged to be the poet's work) without being hurried from one thing to another, as we are in the plays of Calderon, which we have seen lately upon our theatres, under the name of Spanish plots.[4] I have taken notice but of one tragedy of ours, whose plot has that uniformity and unity of design in it which I have commended in the French; and that is *Rollo*[5], or rather, under the name of Rollo, the Story of Bassianus and Geta in Herodian; there indeed the plot is neither large nor intricate, but just enough to fill the minds of the audience, not to cloy them. Besides, you see it founded upon the truth of history, only the time of the action is not reduceable to the strictness of the rules; and you see in some places a little farce mingled, which is below the dignity of the other parts. And in this all our poets are extremely peccant: even Ben Jonson himself, in *Sejanus* and

---

[1] I disbelieve and loathe whatever is exhibited to me in this fashion. (Horace, *Ars Poetica* 188.)

[2] The truth.

[3] Things similar to the truth.

[4] Sir Samuel Tuke's comedy of *The Adventure of Five Hours*, 1663, and the Earl of Bristol's *Elvira, or the Worst not always True*, 1667, were both adaptations from the plays by Calderon.

[5] John Fletcher's tragedy of *The Bloody Brother, or, Rollo, Duke of Normandy*, 1616 (?).

Catiline has given us this oleo of a play, this unnatural mixture of comedy and tragedy, which to me sounds just as ridiculously as the history of David with the merry humours of Golia's. In *Sejanus* you may take notice of the scene betwixt Livia and the physician, which is a pleasant satire upon the artificial helps of beauty: in *Catiline* you may see the parliament of women; the little envies of them to one another; and all that passes betwixt Curio and Fulvia: scenes admirable in their kind, but of an ill mingle with the rest. [...]

'I have observed that in all our tragedies the audience cannot forbear laughing when the actors are to die; 'tis the most comic part of the whole play. All *passions* may be lively represented on the stage if to the well-writing of them the actor supplies a good commanded voice, and limbs that move easily and without stiffness; but there are many *actions* which can never be imitated to a just height. Dying especially is a thing which none but a Roman gladiator could naturally perform on the stage when he did not imitate or represent but do it; and therefore it is better to omit the representation of it. [...]

'As for Jonson, to whose character I am now arrived, if we look upon him while he was himself (for his last plays were but his dotages), I think him the most learned and judicious writer which any theatre ever had. He was a most severe judge of himself as well as others. One cannot say he wanted wit but rather that he was frugal of it. In his works you find little to retrench or alter. Wit and language, and humour also, in some measure we had before him; but something of art was wanting to the drama till he came. He managed his strength to more advantage than any who preceded him. You seldom find him making love in any of his scenes, or endeavouring to move the passions; his genius was too sullen and saturnine to do it gracefully, especially when he knew he came after those who had performed both to such an height. Humour was his proper sphere, and in that he delighted most to represent mechanic people. He was deeply conversant in the ancients, both Greek and Latin, and he borrowed boldly from them; there is scarce a poet or historian among the Roman authors of those times whom he has not translated in *Sejanus* and *Catiline*. But he has done his robberies so openly that one may see he fears not to be taxed by any law. He invades authors like a monarch, and what would be theft in other poets is only victory in him. With the spoils of these writers he so represents old Rome to us, in its rites, ceremonies, and customs, that if one of their poets had written either of his tragedies we had seen less of it than in him. If there was any fault in his language, 'twas that he weaved it too closely and laboriously, in his comedies especially. Perhaps too he did a little too much romanize our tongue, leaving the words which he translated almost as much Latin as he found them; wherein, though he learnedly followed their language, he did not enough comply with the idiom of ours. If I would compare him to Shakespeare, I must acknowledge him the more correct poet but Shakespeare the greater wit. Shakespeare was the Homer, or father of our dramatic poets; Jonson was the Virgil, the pattern of elaborate writing. I admire him, but I love Shakespeare. To conclude of him, as he has given us the most correct plays, so in the precepts which he has laid down in his *Discoveries* we have as many and profitable rules for perfecting the stage as any wherewith the French can furnish us. [...']

THOMAS TRAHERNE

from *The First Century*

29

You never enjoy the world aright till the sea itself floweth in your veins, till you are clothed with the heavens and crowned with the stars, and perceive yourself to be the sole heir of the whole world, and more than so because men are in it who are every one sole heirs as well as you. Till you can sing and rejoice and delight in God as misers do in gold and kings in sceptres you never enjoy the world.

30

Till your spirit filleth the whole world and the stars are your jewels; till you are as familiar with the ways of God in all ages as with your walk and table; till you are intimately acquainted with that shady nothing out of which the world was made; till you love men so as to desire their happiness with a thirst equal to the zeal of your own; till you delight in God for being good to all, you never enjoy the world. Till you more feel it than your private estate, and are more present in the hemisphere, considering the glories and the beauties there, than in your own house; till you remember how lately you were made, and how wonderful it was when you came into it, and more rejoice in the palace of your glory than if it had been made but today morning.

31

Yet further, you never enjoy the world aright till you so love the beauty of enjoying it that you are covetous and earnest to persuade others to enjoy it, and so perfectly hate the abominable corruption of men in despising it that you had rather suffer the flames of hell than willingly be guilty of their error. There is so much blindness and ingratitude and damned folly in it. The world is a mirror of infinite beauty, yet no man sees it. It is a temple of majesty yet no man regards it. It is a region of light and peace, did not men disquiet it. It is the paradise of God. It is more to man since he is fallen than it was before. It is the place of angels and the gate of heaven. When Jacob waked out of his dream he said, 'God is here and I wist it not. How dreadful is this place! This is none other than the house of God and the gate of heaven.'

from *The Second Century*

40

In all love there is a love begetting, a love begotten and a love proceeding. Which though they are one in essence subsist nevertheless in three several manners. For love is benevolent affection to another, which is of itself, and by itself relateth to its object. It floweth from itself and resteth in its object. Love proceedeth of necessity from itself, for unless it be of itself it is not love. Constraint is destructive and opposite to its nature. The love from which it floweth is the fountain of love; the love which streameth from it is the communication of love, or love communicated; and the love which resteth in the object is the love which streameth to it. So that in all love the trinity is clear. By secret passages without stirring it proceedeth to its object, and is as powerfully present as if it did not proceed at all, the love that lieth in the bosom of the lover being the love that is perceived in the spirit of the beloved; that is, the same in substance, though in the manner of substance or subsistence, different. Love in the bosom is the parent of love; love in the stream is the effect of love; love seen, or dwelling in the object, proceedeth from both. Yet are all three one and the self-same love, though three loves.

47

What life can be more pleasant than that which is delighted in itself and in all its objects, in which also all objects infinitely delight? What life can be more pleasant than that which is blessed in all and glorious before all? Now this life is the life of love. For this end therefore did He desire to love that He might be love; infinitely delightful to all objects, infinitely delighted in all, and infinitely pleased in Himself for being delightful to all, and delighted in all. All this He attaineth by love. For love is the most delightful of all employments; all the objects of love are delightful to it, and love is delightful to all its objects. Well then may love be the end of loving, which is so complete; it being a thing so delightful that God infinitely rejoiceth in Himself for being love. And thus you see how God is the end of Himself. He doth what He doth that He may be what He is: wise and glorious and bountiful and blessed in being perfect love.

48

Love is so divine and perfect a thing that it is worthy to be the very end and being of the Deity. It is His goodness, and it is His glory. We therefore so vastly delight in love because all these excellencies and all other whatsoever lie within it. By loving a soul does propagate and beget itself. By loving it does dilate and magnify itself. By loving it does enlarge and delight itself. By loving also it delighteth others, as by loving it doth honour and enrich itself. But above all, by loving it does attain itself, love also being the end of souls, which are never perfect till they are in act what they are in power. They were made to love and are dark and vain and comfortless till they do it. Till they love they are idle or misemployed. Till they love they are desolate, without their objects, and narrow and little and dishonourable: but when they shine by love upon all objects they are accompanied with them and enlightened by them. Till we become therefore all act as God is, we can never rest, nor ever be satisfied.

65

You are as prone to love as the sun is to shine, it being the most delightful and natural employment of the soul of man, without which you are dark and miserable. Consider therefore the extent of love, its vigour and excellency. For certainly he that delights not in love makes vain the universe, and is of necessity to himself the greatest burden. The whole world ministers to you as the theatre of your love. It sustains you and all objects that you may continue to love them, without which it were better for you to have no being. Life without objects is sensible emptiness. Objects without love are the delusion of life. The objects of love are its greatest treasures, and without love it is impossible they should be treasures. For the objects which we love are the pleasing objects, and delightful things. And whatsoever is not pleasing and delightful to us can be no treasure. Nay, it is distasteful, and worse than nothing, since we had rather it should have no being.

from *The Third Century*

5

Our Saviour's meaning when He said, 'He must be born again and become a little child that will enter into the kingdom of heaven' is deeper far than is generally believed. It is not only in a careless reliance upon divine providence that we are to become little children, or in the feebleness and shortness of our anger and simplicity of our passions; but in the peace and purity of all our soul. Which purity also is a deeper thing than is commonly apprehended; for we must disrobe ourselves of all false colours, and unclothe our souls of evil habits; all our thoughts must be infant-like and clear, the powers of our soul free from the leaven of this world, and disentangled from men's conceits and customs. Grit in the eye or the yellow jaundice will not let a man see those objects truly that are before it. And therefore it is requisite that we should be as very strangers to the thoughts, customs and opinions of men in this world, as if we were but little children when they are first born. Ambitions, trades, luxuries, inordinate affections, casual and accidental riches invented since the fall would be gone, and only those things appear which did to Adam in paradise, in the same light, love in our parents, men, ourselves, and the face of heaven. Every man naturally seeing those things to the enjoyment of which he is naturally born.

16

Once I remember (I think I was about four years old) when I thus reasoned with myself, sitting in a little obscure room in my father's poor house. If there be a God certainly He must be infinite in goodness. And that I was prompted to by a real whispering instinct of nature. And if

He be infinite in goodness and a perfect Being in wisdom and love, certainly He must do most glorious things, and give us infinite riches. How comes it to pass therefore that I am so poor, of so scanty and narrow a fortune, enjoying few and obscure comforts? I thought I could not believe Him a God to me unless all His power were employed to glorify me. I knew not then my soul or body, nor did I think of the heavens and the earth, the rivers and the stars, the sun or the seas; all those were lost and absent from me. But when I found them made out of nothing for me, then I had a God indeed, whom I could praise and rejoice in.

46

When I came into the country, and being seated among silent trees, had all my time in mine own hands, I resolved to spend it all, whatever it cost me, in search of happiness, and to satiate that burning thirst which nature had enkindled in me from my youth. In which I was so resolute that I chose rather to live upon £10 a year and to go in leather clothes and feed upon bread and water, so that I might have all my time clearly to myself, than to keep many thousands per annum in an estate of life where my time would be devoured in care and labour. And God was so pleased to accept of that desire that from that time to this I have had all things plentifully provided for me, without any care at all, my very study of felicity making me more to prosper than all the care in the whole world. So that through His blessing I live a free and kingly life, as if the world were turned again into Eden, or much more, as it is at this day.

OLIVER GOLDSMITH

The Double Transformation
A Tale

Secluded from domestic strife,
Jack Bookworm led a college life;
A fellowship at twenty-five,
Made him the happiest man alive;
He drank his glass, and cracked his joke,
And freshmen wondered as he spoke.

  Such pleasures, unalloyed with care,
Could any accident impair?
Could Cupid's shaft at length transfix
Our swain, arrived at thirty-six?
Oh! had the archer ne'er come down
To ravage in a country town,
Or Flavia been content to stop
At triumphs in a Fleet Street shop:
Oh! had her eyes forgot to blaze,
Or Jack had wanted eyes to gaze!
Oh! – But let exclamation cease,
Her presence banished all his peace:
So with decorum all things carried,
Miss frowned, and blushed, and then was – married.
Need we expose to vulgar sight
The raptures of the bridal night?
Need we intrude on hallowed ground,
Or draw the curtains closed around?
Let it suffice, that each had charms:
He clasped a goddess in his arms;
And though she felt his visage rough,
Yet in a man 'twas well enough.

  The honey-moon like lightning flew;
The second brought its transports too;
A third, a fourth, were not amiss;
The fifth was friendship mixed with bliss:
But when a twelvemonth passed away,
Jack found his goddess made of clay;
Found half the charms that decked her face
Arose from powder, shreds, or lace:

But still the worst remained behind,
That very face had robbed her mind.
  Skilled in no other arts was she,
But dressing, patching, repartee;
And, just as humour rose or fell,
By turns a slattern or a belle;
'Tis true she dressed with modern grace,
Half naked at a ball or race;
But when at home, at board or bed,
Five greasy nightcaps wrapped her head.
Could so much beauty condescend
To be a dull domestic friend?
Could any curtain lectures bring
To decency so fine a thing?
In short, by night, 'twas fits or fretting;
By day, 'twas gadding or coquetting.
Fond to be seen, she kept a bevy
Of powdered coxcombs at her levee:
The squire and captain too their stations,
And twenty other near relations:
Jack sucked his pipe and often broke
A sigh in suffocating smoke;
While all their hours were passed between
Insulting repartee or spleen.
  Thus as her faults each day were known,
He thinks her features coarser grown;
He fancies every vice she shows,
Or thins her lip or points her nose:
Whenever rage or envy rise,
How wide her mouth, how wild her eyes?
He knows not how, but so it is,
Her face is grown a knowing phiz;
And, though her fops are wondrous civil,
He thinks her ugly as the devil.
  Now, to perplex the ravelled noose,
As each a different way pursues,
While sullen or loquacious strife
Promised to hold them on for life,
That dire disease, whose ruthless power
Withers the beauty's transient flower,
Lo! the small-pox, with horrid glare
Levelled its terrors at the fair;

And, rifling every youthful grace,
Left but the remnant of a face.
    The glass, grown hateful to her sight,
Reflected now a perfect fright;
Each former art she vainly tries
To bring back lustre to her eyes.
In vain she tries her pastes and creams,
To smooth her skin, or hide its seams;
Her country beaux and city cousins,
Lovers no more, flew off by dozens;
The squire himself was seen to yield,
And even the captain quit the field.
    Poor madam, now condemned to hack
The rest of life with anxious Jack,
Perceiving others fairly flown,
Attempted pleasing him alone.
Jack soon was dazzled to behold
Her present face surpass the old;
With modesty her cheeks are dyed,
Humility displaces pride;
For tawdry finery is seen
A person ever neatly clean;
No more presuming on her sway,
She learns good-nature every day:
Serenely gay, and strict in duty,
Jack finds his wife a perfect beauty.

An Elegy on the Death of a Mad Dog

Good people all, of every sort,
    Give ear unto my song;
And if you find it wondrous short,
    It cannot hold you long.

In Islington there was a man,
    Of whom the world might say,
That still a godly race he ran,
    Whene'er he went to pray.

A kind and gentle heart he had,
　　To comfort friends and foes;
The naked every day he clad,
　　When he put on his clothes.

And in that town a dog was found,
　　As many dogs there be,
Both mongrel, puppy, whelp, and hound,
　　And curs of low degree.

This dog and man at first were friends;
　　But when a pique began,
The dog, to gain some private ends,
　　Went mad and bit the man.

Around from all the neighbouring streets
　　The wondering neighbours ran,
And swore the dog had lost his wits,
　　To bite so good a man.

The wound it seemed both sore and sad
　　To every Christian eye;
And while they swore the dog was mad,
　　They swore the man would die.

But soon a wonder came to light,
　　That showed the rogues they lied;
The man recovered of the bite,
　　The dog it was that died.

Stanzas on Woman

When lovely woman stoops to folly,
　　And finds too late that men betray,
What charm can soothe her melancholy,
　　What art can wash her guilt away?

The only art her guilt to cover,
　　To hide her shame from every eye,
To give repentance to her lover,
And wring his bosom – is, to die.

The Citizen of the World

LETTER XCIII
The fondness of some, to admire the writing of lords, &c.

It is surprizing what an influence titles shall have upon the mind, even though these titles be of our own making. Like children we dress up the puppets in finery, and then stand in astonishment at the plastic wonder. I have been told of a rat-catcher here, who strolled for a long time about the villages near town, without finding any employment; at last, however, he thought proper to take the title of his Majesty's Rat-catcher in ordinary, and this succeeded beyond his expectations; when it was known that he caught rats at court, all were ready to give him countenance and employment.

But of all the people, they who make books seem most perfectly sensible of the advantage of titular dignity. All seem convinced, that a book written by vulgar hands, can neither instruct nor improve; none but Kings, Chams, and Mandarines, can write with any probability of success. If the titles inform me right, not only Kings and Courtiers, but Emperors themselves in this country, periodically supply the press.

A man here who should write, and honestly confess that he wrote for bread, might as well send his manuscript to fire the baker's oven; not one creature will read him; all must be court-bred poets, or pretend at least to be court-bred, who can expect to please. Should the caitiff fairly avow a design of emptying our pockets and filling his own, every reader would instantly forsake him; even those, who write for bread themselves, would combine to worry him, perfectly sensible, that his attempts only served to take the bread out of their mouths.

And yet this silly prepossession the more amazes me, when I consider, that almost all the excellent productions in wit that have appeared here, were purely the offspring of necessity; their Drydens, Butlers, Otways, and Farquhars, were all writers for bread. Believe me, my friend, hunger has a most amazing faculty of sharpening the genius; and he who with a full belly, can think like a hero, after a course of fasting, shall rise to the sublimity of a demi-god.

But what will most amaze, is, that this very set of men, who are now so much depreciated by fools, are however the very best writers they have among them at present. For my own part, were I to buy a hat, I would not have it from a stocking-maker, but an hatter; were I to buy shoes, I should not go to the taylor's for that purpose. It is just so with regard to wit: did I, for my life, desire to be well-served, I would apply only to those who made it their trade, and lived by it. You smile at the oddity of my opinion; but be assured, my friend, that wit is in some measure mechanical; and that a man long habituated to catch at even its resemblance, will at last be happy enough to possess the substance: by a long habit of writing he acquires a justness of thinking, and a mastery of manner, which holiday-writers, even with ten times his genius, may vainly attempt to equal.

How then are they deceived, who expect from title, dignity, and exterior circumstance, an excellence, which is in some measure acquired by habit, and sharpened by necessity; you have seen, like me, many literary reputations promoted by the influence of fashion, which have scarce survived the possessor; you have seen the poor hardly earn the little reputation they acquired, and their merit only acknowledged when they were incapable of enjoying the pleasures of popularity; such, however, is the reputation worth possessing, that which is hardly earned is hardly lost. Adieu.

WILLIAM BLAKE

Songs of Innocence

INTRODUCTION

Piping down the valleys wild,
Piping songs of pleasant glee,
On a cloud I saw a child,
And he laughing said to me:

'Pipe a song about a Lamb.'
So I piped with merry chear.
'Piper, pipe that song again.'
So I piped, he wept to hear.

'Drop thy pipe, thy happy pipe,
Sing thy songs of happy chear.'
So I sung the same again,
While he wept with joy to hear.

'Piper, sit thee down and write
In a book that all may read.'
So he vanish'd from my sight.
And I pluck'd a hollow reed,

And I made a rural pen,
And I stain'd the water clear,
And I wrote my happy songs
Every child may joy to hear.

THE LITTLE BLACK BOY

My mother bore me in the southern wild,
And I am black, but O! my soul is white;
White as an angel is the English child,
But I am black, as if bereav'd of light.

My mother taught me underneath a tree,
And sitting down before the heat of day
She took me on her lap and kissed me,
And pointing to the east began to say:

'Look on the rising sun: there God does live,
And gives his light and gives his heat away;
And flowers and trees and beasts and men receive
Comfort in morning, joy in the noon day.

'And we are put on earth a little space,
That we may learn to bear the beams of love;
And these black bodies and this sun-burnt face
Is but a cloud, and like a shady grove.

'For when our souls have learn'd the heat to bear,
The cloud will vanish; we shall hear his voice,
Saying: "Come out from the grove, my love & care,
And round my golden tent like lambs rejoice." '

Thus did my mother say, and kissed me;
And thus I say to little English boy:
When I from black and he from white cloud free
And round the tent of God like lambs we joy,

I'll shade him from the heat, till he can bear
To lean in joy upon our father's knee;
And then I'll stand and stroke his silver hair,
And be like him, and he will then love me.

A CRADLE SONG

Sweet dreams, form a shade
O'er my lovely infant's head,
Sweet dreams of pleasant streams
By happy silent moony beams.

Sweet sleep, with soft down
Weave thy brows an infant crown.
Sweet sleep, Angel mild,
Hover o'er my happy child.

Sweet smiles, in the night
Hover over my delight.
Sweet smiles, Mother's smiles,
All the livelong night beguiles.

Sweet moans, dovelike sighs,
Chase not slumber from thy eyes.
Sweet moans, sweeter smiles,
All the dovelike moans beguiles.

Sleep, sleep, happy child.
All creation slept and smil'd.
Sleep, sleep, happy sleep,
While o'er thee thy mother weep.

THE DIVINE IMAGE

To Mercy, Pity, Peace and Love
All pray in their distress;
And to these virtues of delight
Return their thankfulness.

For Mercy, Pity, Peace and Love
Is God, our father dear,
And Mercy, Pity, Peace and Love
Is Man, his child and care.

For Mercy has a human heart,
Pity, a human face,
And Love, the human form divine,
And Peace, the human dress.

Then every man of every clime
That prays in his distress,
Prays to the human form divine:
Love, Mercy, Pity, Peace.

And all must love the human form
In heathen, turk or jew.
Where Mrcy, Love & Pity dwell
There God is dwelling too.

NURSE'S SONG

When the voices of children are heard on the green
And laughing is heard on the hill,
My heart is at rest within my breast
And every thing else is still.

'Then come home, my children, the sun is gone down
And the dews of night arise;
Come, come, leave off play, and let us away
Till the morning appears in the skies.'

'No, no, let us play, for it is yet day
And we cannot go to sleep;
Besides, in the sky the little birds fly
And the hills are all cover'd with sheep.'

'Well, well, go & play till the light fades away
And then go home to bed.'
The little ones leaped & shouted & laugh'd
And all the hills ecchoed.

Songs of Experience

HOLY THURSDAY

Is this a holy thing to see
In a rich and fruitful land,
Babes reduc'd to misery,
Fed with cold and usurous hand?

Is that trembling cry a song?
Can it be a song of joy?
And so many children poor?
It is a land of poverty!

And their sun does never shine,
And their fields are bleak & bare,
And their ways are fill'd with thorns;
It is eternal winter there.

For where-e'r the sun does shine,
And where-e'r the rain does fall,
Babe can never hunger there,
Nor poverty the mind appall.

THE SICK ROSE

O Rose, thou art sick.
The invisible worm,
That flies in the night
In the howling storm,

Has found out thy bed
Of crimson joy;
And his dark secret love
Does thy life destroy.

THE TYGER

Tyger, Tyger, burning bright
In the forests of the night,
What immortal hand or eye
Could frame thy fearful symmetry?

In what distant deeps or skies
Burnt the fire of thine eyes?
On what wings dare he aspire?
What the hand dare seize the fire?

And what shoulder, & what art,
Could twist the sinews of thy heart?
And when thy heart began to beat,
What dread hand? & what dread feet?

What the hammer? what the chain?
In what furnace was thy brain?
What the anvil? what dread grasp
Dare its deadly terrors clasp?

When the stars threw down their spears
And water'd heaven with their tears,
Did he smile his work to see?
Did he who made the Lamb make thee?

Tyger, Tyger, burning bright
In the forests of the night,
What immortal hand or eye
Dare frame thy fearful symmetry?

AH! SUN-FLOWER

Ah, Sun-flower! weary of time,
Who countest the steps of the Sun,
Seeking after that sweet golden clime
Where the traveller's journey is done;

Where the Youth pined away with desire,
And the pale Virgin shrouded in snow,
Arise from their graves and aspire
Where my Sun-flower wishes to go.

A POISON TREE

I was angry with my friend;
I told my wrath, my wrath did end.
I was angry with my foe;
I told it not, my wrath did grow.

And I water'd it in fears,
Night & morning with my tears;
And I sunned it with smiles,
And with soft deceitful wiles.

And it grew both day and night,
Till it bore an apple bright;
And my foe beheld it shine,
And he knew that it was mine,

And into my garden stole
When the night had veil'd the pole.
In the morning glad I see
My foe outstretch'd beneath the tree.

WILLIAM WORDSWORTH

Lines written a few miles above Tintern Abbey

On revisiting the banks of the Wye during a tour
July 13, 1798

Five years have passed; five summers, with the length
Of five long winters! and again I hear
These waters, rolling from their mountain-springs
With a sweet inland murmur. Once again
Do I behold these steep and lofty cliffs,
Which on a wild secluded scene impress
Thoughts of more deep seclusion, and connect
The landscape with the quiet of the sky.

The day is come when I again repose
Here, under this dark sycamore, and view
These plots of cottage-ground, these orchard-tufts,
Which, at this season, with their unripe fruits,
Among the woods and copses lose themselves,
Nor, with their green and simple hue, disturb
The wild green landscape. Once again I see
These hedge-rows, hardly hedge-rows, little lines
Of sportive wood run wild; these pastoral farms
Green to the very door, and wreaths of smoke
Sent up, in silence, from among the trees,
With some uncertain notice, as might seem,
Of vagrant dwellers in the houseless woods,
Or of some hermit's cave, where by his fire
The hermit sits alone.

               Though absent long,
These forms of beauty have not been to me
As is a landscape to a blind man's eye;
But oft, in lonely rooms, and mid the din
Of towns and cities, I have owed to them,
In hours of weariness, sensations sweet,
Felt in the blood, and felt along the heart,
And passing even into my purer mind
With tranquil restoration; feelings too
Of unremembered pleasure – such, perhaps,
As may have had no trivial influence
On that best portion of a good man's life:
His little, nameless, unremembered acts
Of kindness and of love. Nor less, I trust,
To them I may have owed another gift,
Of aspect more sublime – that blessed mood
In which the burthen of the mystery,
In which the heavy and the weary weight
Of all this unintelligible world
Is lightened; that serene and blessed mood
In which the affections gently lead us on,
Until, the breath of this corporeal frame,
And even the motion of our human blood
Almost suspended, we are laid asleep
In body, and become a living soul,
While with an eye made quiet by the power

Of harmony, and the deep power of joy,
We see into the life of things.

                    If this
Be but a vain belief, yet oh! how oft
In darkness, and amid the many shapes
Of joyless day-light, when the fretful stir
Unprofitable, and the fever of the world
Have hung upon the beatings of my heart,
How oft, in spirit, have I turned to thee
O sylvan Wye! Thou wanderer through the woods,
How often has my spirit turned to thee!

And now, with gleams of half-extinguished thought,
With many recognitions dim and faint,
And somewhat of a sad perplexity,
The picture of the mind revives again
While here I stand, not only with the sense
Of present pleasure, but with pleasing thoughts
That in this moment there is life and food
For future years. And so I dare to hope
Though changed, no doubt, from what I was when first
I came among these hills; when like a roe
I bounded o'er the mountains, by the sides
Of the deep rivers and the lonely streams,
Wherever nature led; more like a man
Flying from something that he dreads, than one
Who sought the thing he loved. For nature then
(The coarser pleasures of my boyish days
And their glad animal movements all gone by)
To me was all in all. I cannot paint
What then I was. The sounding cataract
Haunted me like a passion; the tall rock,
The mountain, and the deep and gloomy wood,
Their colours and their forms, were then to me
An appetite – a feeling and a love
That had no need of a remoter charm,
By thought supplied, or any interest
Unborrowed from the eye. That time is past,
And all its aching joys are now no more,
And all its dizzy raptures. Not for this
Faint I, nor mourn nor murmur: other gifts

Have followed – for such loss, I would believe,
Abundant recompense. For I have learned
To look on nature, not as in the hour
Of thoughtless youth, but hearing oftentimes
The still, sad music of humanity,
Not harsh nor grating, though of ample power
To chasten and subdue. And I have felt
A presence that disturbs me with the joy
Of elevated thoughts: a sense sublime
Of something far more deeply interfused,
Whose dwelling is the light of setting suns,
And the round ocean, and the living air,
And the blue sky, and in the mind of man –
A motion and a spirit that impels
All thinking things, all objects of all thought,
And rolls through all things. Therefore am I still
A lover of the meadows and the woods,
And mountains, and of all that we behold
From this green earth; of all the mighty world
Of eye and ear, both what they half-create,
And what perceive; well pleased to recognize
In Nature and the language of the sense
The anchor of my purest thoughts, the nurse,
The guide, the guardian of my heart, and soul
Of all my moral being.

                Nor, perchance,
If I were not thus taught, should I the more
Suffer my genial spirits to decay:
For thou art with me, here, upon the banks
Of this fair river; thou, my dearest friend,
My dear, dear friend, and in thy voice I catch
The language of my former heart, and read
My former pleasures in the shooting lights
Of thy wild eyes. Oh! yet a little while
May I behold in thee what I was once,
My dear, dear sister! And this prayer I make,
Knowing that Nature never did betray
The heart that loved her; 'tis her privilege,
Through all the years of this our life, to lead
From joy to joy: for she can so inform
The mind that is within us, so impress

With quietness and beauty, and so feed
With lofty thoughts, that neither evil tongues,
Rash judgements, nor the sneers of selfish men,
Nor greetings where no kindness is, nor all
The dreary intercourse of daily life
Shall e'er prevail against us, or disturb
Our cheerful faith that all which we behold
Is full of blessings. Therefore let the moon
Shine on thee in thy solitary walk,
And let the misty mountain winds be free
To blow against thee; and in after years,
When these wild ecstasies shall be matured
Into a sober pleasure, when thy mind
Shall be a mansion for all lovely forms,
Thy memory be as a dwelling-place
For all sweet sounds and harmonies, oh! then,
If solitude, or fear, or pain, or grief,
Should be thy portion, with what healing thoughts
Of tender joy wilt thou remember me,
And these my exhortations! Nor, perchance,
If I should be where I no more can hear
Thy voice, nor catch from thy wild eyes these gleams
Of past existence, wilt thou then forget
That on the banks of this delightful stream
We stood together, and that I, so long
A worshipper of Nature, hither came
Unwearied in that service – rather say
With warmer love, oh! with far deeper zeal
Of holier love. Nor wilt thou then forget,
That after many wanderings, many years
Of absence, these steep woods and lofty cliffs,
And this green pastoral landscape, were to me
More dear, both for themselves, and for thy sake.

Song

She dwelt among th' untrodden ways
    Beside the springs of Dove:
A maid whom there were none to praise
    And very few to love.

A violet by a mossy stone
    Half hidden from the eye!
– Fair as a star when only one
    Is shining in the sky!

She lived unknown, and few could know
    When Lucy ceased to be;
But she is in her grave, and oh!
    The difference to me.

'A slumber did my spirit seal'

A slumber did my spirit seal,
    I had no human fears;
She seemed a thing that could not feel
    The touch of earthly years.

No motion has she now, no force;
    She neither hears nor sees,
Rolled round in earth's diurnal course
    With rocks and stones and trees!

Composed Upon Westminster Bridge
Sept. 3, 1803

Earth has not any thing to show more fair;
Dull would he be of soul who could pass by
A sight so touching in its majesty.
This city now doth like a garment wear

The beauty of the morning; silent, bare,
Ships, towers, domes, theatres, and temples lie
Open unto the fields, and to the sky,
All bright and glittering in the smokeless air.
Never did sun more beautifully steep
In his first splendour valley, rock, or hill;
Ne'er saw I, never felt, a calm so deep!
The river glideth at his own sweet will;
Dear God! the very houses seem asleep,
And all that mighty heart is lying still!

'It is a beauteous evening, calm and free'

It is a beauteous evening, calm and free;
The holy time is quiet as a nun
Breathless with adoration; the broad sun
Is sinking down in its tranquillity;
The gentleness of heaven is on the sea.
Listen! the mighty being is awake
And doth with his eternal motion make
A sound like thunder – everlastingly.
Dear child! dear girl! that walkest with me here,
If thou appear'st untouched by solemn thought,
Thy nature is not therefore less divine:
Thou liest in Abraham's bosom all the year,
And worship'st at the temple's inner shrine,
God being with thee when we know it not.

'Surprised by joy, impatient as the wind'

Surprised by joy, impatient as the wind,
I wished to share the transport – oh! with whom
But thee, long buried in the silent tomb,
That spot which no vicissitude can find?
Love, faithful love, recalled thee to my mind,
But how could I forget thee? Through what power,

Even for the least division of an hour,
Have I been so beguiled as to be blind
To my most grievous loss? That thought's return
Was the worst pang that sorrow ever bore,
Save one – one only – when I stood forlorn,
Knowing my heart's best treasure was no more:
That neither present time, nor years unborn
Could to my sight that heavenly face restore.
With songs the budded groves resounding;
And to my heart is still endeared
The faith with which it then was cheered –
The faith which saw that gladsome pair
Walk through the fire with unsinged hair.
Of, if such thoughts must needs deceive,
Kind spirits! may we not believe
That they, so happy and so fair,
Through your sweet influence, and the care
Of pitying heaven, at least were free
From touch of *deadly* injury?
Destined, whate'er their earthly doom,
For mercy and immortal bloom!

from the Preface to *Lyrical Ballads* (1802)

[…] Not that I mean to say, that I always began to write with a distinct purpose formally conceived; but I believe that my habits of meditation have so formed my feelings, as that my descriptions of such objects as strongly excite those feelings, will be found to carry along with them a *purpose*. If in this opinion I am mistaken, I can have little right to the name of a Poet. For all good poetry is the spontaneous overflow of powerful feelings: but though this be true, Poems to which any value can be attached, were never produced on any variety of subjects but by a man, who being possessed of more than usual organic sensibility, had also thought long and deeply. For our continued influxes of feeling are modified and directed by our thoughts, which are indeed the representatives of all our past feelings; and, as by contemplating the relation of these general representatives to each other we discover what is really important to men, so, by the repetition and continuance of this act, our feelings will be connected with important subjects, till at length, if we be originally possessed of much sensibility, such habits of mind will be produced, that, by obeying blindly and mechanically the impulses of those habits, we shall describe objects, and utter sentiments, of such a nature and in such connection with each other, that the understanding of the being to whom we address ourselves, if he be in a healthful state of association, must necessarily be in some degree enlightened, and his affections ameliorated.

[...] There will also be found in these volumes little of what is usually called poetic diction; I have taken as much pains to avoid it as others ordinarily take to produce it; this I have done for the reason already alleged, to bring my language near to the language of men, and further, because the pleasure which I have proposed to myself to impart is of a kind very different from that which is supposed by many persons to be the proper object of poetry. I do not know how, without being culpably particular, I can give my Reader a more exact notion of the style in which I wished these poems to be written than by informing him that I have at all times endeavoured to look steadily at my subject, consequently, I hope that there is in these Poems little falsehood of description, and that my ideas are expressed in language fitted to their respective importance. Something I must have gained by this practice, as it is friendly to one property of all good poetry, namely good sense; but it has necessarily cut me off from a large portion of phrases and figures of speech which from father to son have long been regarded as the common inheritance of Poets. I have also thought it expedient to restrict myself still further, having abstained from the use of many expressions, in themselves proper and beautiful, but which have been foolishly repeated by bad Poets, till such feelings of disgust are connected with them as it is scarcely possible by any art of association to overpower.

SAMUEL TAYLOR COLERIDGE

from *The Rime of the Ancient Mariner*

PART I

It is an ancient Mariner,
   And he stoppeth one of three.
'By thy long grey beard and glittering eye,
   Now wherefore stopp'st thou me?

The Bridegroom's doors are opened wide
   And I am next of kin;
The guests are met, the feast is set: –
   May'st hear the merry din.'

But still he holds the Wedding-Guest –
   'There was a ship,' quoth he –
'Nay, it thou'st got a laughsome tale,
   Mariner! come with me.'

He holds him with his skinny hand,
   Quoth he, 'there was a Ship' –
'Now get thee hence, thou grey-beard loon!
   Or my Staff shall make thee skip.'

He holds him with his glittering eye –
   The Wedding-Guest stood still,
And listens like a three years' child:
   The Mariner hath his will.

The Wedding-Guest sat on a stone:
   He cannot choose but hear;
And thus spake on that ancient man,
   The bright-eyed Mariner.

'The ship was cheered, the harbour cleared,
   Merrily did we drop
Below the kirk, below the hill,
   Below the lighthouse top.

The Sun came up upon the left,
    Out of the sea came he!
And he shone bright, and on the right
    Went down into the sea.

Higher and higher every day,
    Till over the mast at noon' –
The Wedding-Guest here beat his breast,
    For he heard the loud bassoon.

The bride hath paced into the hall,
    Red as a rose is she;
Nodding their heads before her goes
    The merry minstrelsy.

The Wedding-Guest he beat his breast,
    Yet he cannot choose but hear;
And thus spake on that ancient man,
    The bright-eyed Mariner.

'Listen, Stranger! Storm and Wind,
    A Wind and Tempest strong!
For days and weeks it play'd us freaks –
    Like chaff we drove along.

With sloping masts and dipping prow,
    As who pursued with yell and blow
    Still treads the shadow of his foe,
And forward bends his head,
    The ship drove fast, loud roared the blast,
And southward aye we fled.

And now there came both mist and snow,
    And it grew wondrous cold:
And ice, mast-high, came floating by
    As green as emerald.

And through the drifts the snowy clifts
    Did send a dismal sheen:
Nor shapes of men nor beasts we ken –
    The ice was all between.

The ice was here, the ice was there,
    The ice was all around:
It cracked and growled, and roared and howled,
    Like noises in a swound!

At length did cross an Albatross,
    Thorough the fog it came;
As if it had been a Christian soul,
    We hailed it in God's name.

The mariners gave it biscuit-worms,
    And round and round it flew.
The ice did split with a thunder-fit;
    The helmsman steered us through!

And a good south wind sprung up behind;
    The Albatross did follow,
And every day, for food or play,
    Came to the mariner's hollo!

In mist or cloud, on mast or shroud,
    It perched for vespers nine;
Whiles all the night, through fog-smoke white,
    Glimmered the white Moon-shine.'

'God save thee, ancient Mariner!
    From the fiends, that plague thee thus! –
Why look'st thou so?' – With my cross-bow
    I shot the Albatross.

PART II

The Sun came up upon the right,
    Out of the sea came he;
And broad as a weft upon the left
    Went down into the sea.

And the good south wind still blew behind,
    But no sweet bird did follow,
Nor any day for food or play
    Came to the mariners' hollo!

And I had done a hellish thing,
  And it would work 'em woe:
For all averred, I had killed the bird
  That made the breeze to blow.
Ah wretch! said they, the bird to slay,
  That made the breeze to blow!

Nor dim nor red, like God's own head,
  The glorious Sun uprist:
Then all averred, I had killed the bird
  That brought the fog and mist.
'Twas right, said that, such birds to slay,
  That bring the fog and mist.

The fair breeze blew, the white foam flew,
  The furrow followed free;
We were the first that ever burst
  Into that silent sea.

Down dropt the breeze, the sails dropt down,
  'Twas sad as sad could be;
And we did speak only to break
  The silence of the sea!

All in a hot and copper sky,
  The bloody Sun, at noon,
Right up above the mast did stand,
  No bigger than the Moon.

Day after day, day after day,
  We stuck, nor breath nor motion;
As idle as a painted ship
  Upon a painted ocean.

Water, water, every where,
  And all the boards did shrink;
Water, water, every where,
  Nor any drop to drink.

The very deep did rot: O Christ!
  That ever this should be!
Yea, slimy things did crawl with legs
  Upon the slimy sea.

About, about, in reel and rout
  The death-fires danced at night;
The water, like a witch's oils,
  Burnt green, and blue and white.

And some in dreams assuréd were
  Of the Spirit that plagues us so;
Nine fathom deep he had followed us
  From the land of mist and snow.

And every tongue, through utter drought,
  Was withered at the root;
We could not speak, no more than if
  We had been choked with soot.

Ah! well a-day! what evil looks
  Had I from old and young!
Instead of the cross, the Albatross
  About my neck was hung.

PART V

Oh sleep! it is a gentle thing,
  Beloved from pole to pole!
To Mary Queen the praise be given!
She sent the gentle sleep from Heaven,
  That slid into my soul.

The silly buckets on the deck,
  That had so long remained,
I dreamt that they were filled with dew;
  And when I awoke, it rained.

My lips were wet, my throat was cold,
  My garments all were dank;
Sure I had drunken in my dreams,
  And still my body drank.

I moved, and could not feel my limbs:
  I was so light – almost
I thought that I had died in sleep,
  And was a blesséd ghost.

And soon I heard a roaring wind:
    It did not come anear;
But with its sound it shook the sails,
    That were so thin and sere.

The upper air burst into life!
    And a hundred fire-flags sheen,
To and fro they were hurried about!
And to and fro, and in and out,
    The wan stars danced between.

And the coming wind did roar more loud,
    And the sails did sigh like sedge;
And the rain poured down from one black cloud;
    The Moon was at its edge.

The thick black cloud was cleft, and still
    The Moon was at its side:
Like waters shot from some high crag,
The lightning fell with never a jag,
    A river steep and wide.

The strong wind reach'd the ship: it roar'd
    And dropp'd down, like a stone!
Beneath the lightning and the Moon
    The dead men gave a groan.

They groaned, they stirred, they all uprose,
    Nor spake, nor moved their eyes;
It had been strange, even in a dream,
    To have seen those dead men rise.

The helmsman steered, the ship moved on;
    Yet never a breeze up-blew;
The mariners all 'gan work the ropes,
    Where they were wont to do;
They raised their limbs like lifeless tools –
    We were a ghastly crew.

The body of my brother's son
    Stood by me, knee to knee:
The body and I pulled at one rope,

But he said nought to me.
And I quak'd to think of my own voice
   How frightful it would be!

'I fear thee, ancient Mariner!'
   Be calm, thou wedding-guest!
'Twas not those souls, that fled in pain,
Which to their corses came again,
   But a troop of Spirits blest.

For when it dawned – they dropped their arms,
   And clustered round the mast:
Sweet sounds rose slowly through their mouths,
   And from their bodies passed.

Around, around, flew each sweet sound,
   Then darted to the Sun;
Slowly the sounds came back again,
   Now mixed, now one by one.

Sometimes a-dropping from the sky
   I heard the sky-lark sing;
Sometimes all little birds that are,
How they seemed to fill the sea and air
   With their sweet jargoning!

And now 'twas like all instruments,
   Now like a lonely flute;
And now it is an angel's song,
   That makes the heavens be mute.

It ceased; yet still the sails made on
   A pleasant noise till noon,
A noise like of a hidden brook
   In the leafy month of June,
That to the sleeping woods all night
   Singeth a quiet tune.

Listen, O listen, thou Wedding-Guest!
   'Mariner! thou hast thy will:
For that, which comes out of thine eye, doth make
   My body and soul to be still.'

Never sadder tale was told
    To a man of woman born:
Sadder and wiser thou Wedding-Guest!
    Thou'lt rise tomorrow morn.

Never sadder tale was heard
    By man of woman born:
The mariners all return'd to work
    As silent as beforne.

The mariners all 'gan pull the ropes,
    But look at me they n'old:
Thought I, I am as thin as air –
    They cannot me behold.

Till noon we quietly sailed on,
    Yet never a breeze did breathe:
Slowly and smoothly went the ship,
    Moved onward from beneath.

Under the keel nine fathom deep,
    From the land of mist and snow,
The spirit slid: and it was he
    That made the ship to go.
The sails at noon left off their tune,
    And the ship stood still also.

The Sun, right up above the mast,
    Had fixed her to the ocean:
But in a minute she 'gan stir,
    With a short uneasy motion –
Backwards and forwards half her length
    With a short uneasy motion.

Then like a pawing horse let go,
    She made a sudden bound:
It flung the blood into my head,
    And I fell down in a swound.

How long in that same fit I lay,
    I have not to declare:
But ere my living life returned,

I heard and in my soul discerned
    Two voices in the air.

'Is it he?' quoth one, 'Is this the man?
    By him who died on cross,
With his cruel bow he laid full low
    The harmless Albatross.

The spirit who bideth by himself
    In the land of mist and snow,
He loved the bird that loved the man
    Who shot him with his bow.'

The other was a softer voice,
    As sot as honey-dew:
Quoth he, 'The man hath penance done,
    And penance more will do.'

PART VII

This Hermit good lives in that wood
    Which slopes down to the sea.
How loudly his sweet voice he rears!
He loves to talk with marineres
    That come from a far countree.

He kneels at morn, and noon, and eve –
    He hath a cushion plump:
It is the moss that wholly hides
    The rotted old oak-stump.

The skiff-boat neared: I heard them talk,
    'Why, this is strange, I trow!
Where are those lights so many and fair,
    That signal made but now?'

'Strange, by my faith!' the Hermit said –
    'And they answered not our cheer!
The planks look warped! and see those sails,
    How thin they are and sere!
I never saw aught like to them,
    Unless perchance it were

Brown skeletons of leaves that lag
    My forest-brook along;
When the ivy-tod is heavy with snow,
And the owlet whoops to the wolf below,
    That eats the she-wolf's young.'

'Dear Lord! it hath a fiendish look –'
    (The Pilot made reply)
'I am a-feared' – 'Push on, push on!'
    Said the Hermit cheerily.

The boat came closer to the ship,
    But I nor spake nor stirred;
The boat came close beneath the ship,
    And straight a sound was heard.

Under the water it rumbled on,
    Still louder and more dread:
It reached the ship, it split the bay;
    The ship went down like lead.

Stunned by that loud and dreadful sound,
    Which sky and ocean smote,
Like one that hath been seven days drowned
    My body lay afloat;
But swift as dreams, myself I found
    Within the Pilot's boat.

Upon the whirl, where sank the ship,
    The boat spun round and round;
And all was still, save that the hill
    Was telling of the sound.

I moved my lips – the Pilot shrieked
    And fell down in a fit;
The holy Hermit raised his eyes,
    And prayed where he did sit.

I took the oars: the Pilot's boy,
    Who now doth crazy go,
Laughed loud and long, and all the while
    His eyes went to and fro.

'Ha! ha!' quoth he, 'full plain I see,
    The Devil knows how to row.'

And now all in my own countree,
    I stood on the firm land!
The Hermit stepped forth from the boat,
    And scarcely he could stand.

'O shrieve me, shrieve me, holy man!'
    The Hermit crossed his brow.
'Say quick,' quoth he, 'I bid thee say –
    What manner of man art thou?'

Forthwith this frame of mine was wrenched
    With a woeful agony,
Which forced me to begin my tale;
    And then it left me free.

Since then, at an uncertain hour,
    That agony returns:
And till my ghastly tale is told,
    This heart within me burns.

I pass, like night, from land to land;
    I have strange power of speech;
That moment that his face I see,
I know the man that must hear me:
    To him my tale I teach.

What loud uproar bursts from that door!
    The wedding-guests are there:
But in the garden-bower the bride
    And bride-maids singing are:
And hark the little vesper bell
    Which biddeth me to prayer!

O Wedding-Guest! this soul hath been
    Alone on a wide wide sea:
So lonely 'twas, that God himself
    Scarce seeméd there to be.

O sweeter than the marriage-feast,
   'Tis sweeter far to me,
To walk together to the kirk
   With a goodly company! –

To walk together to the kirk,
   And all together pray,
While each to his great Father bends,
Old men, and babes, and loving friends
   And youths and maidens gay!

Farewell, farewell! but this I tell
   To thee, thou Wedding-Guest!
He prayeth well, who loveth well
   Both man and bird and beast.

He prayeth best, who loveth best
   All things both great and small;
For the dear God who loveth us,
   He made and loveth all.

The Mariner, whose eye is bright,
   Whose beard with age is hoar,
Is gone: and now the Wedding-Guest
   Turned from the bridegroom's door.

He went like one that hath been stunned,
   And is of sense forlorn:
A sadder and a wiser man,
   He rose the morrow morn.

Frost at Midnight

The Frost performs its secret ministry,
Unhelped by any wind. The owlet's cry
Came loud – and hark, again! loud as before.
The inmates of my cottage, all at rest,
Have left me to that solitude, which suits
Abstruser musings: save that at my side

My cradled infant slumbers peacefully.
'Tis calm indeed! so calm, that it disturbs
And vexes meditation with its strange
And extreme silentness. Sea, hill, and wood,
This populous village! Sea, and hill, and wood,
With all the numberless goings-on of life,
Inaudible as dreams! the thin blue flame
Lies on my low-burnt fire, and quivers not;
Only that film, which fluttered on the grate,
Still flutters there, the sole unquiet thing.
Methinks, its motion in this hush of nature
Gives it dim sympathies with me who live,
Making it a companionable form,
Whose puny flaps and freaks the idling Spirit
By its own moods interprets, every where
Echo or mirror seeking of itself,
And makes a toy of Thought.

                                But O! how soft,
How oft, at school, with most believing mind,
Presageful, have I gazed upon the bars,
To watch that fluttering *stranger*! and as oft
With unclosed lids, already had I dreamt
Of my sweet birth-place, and the old church-tower,
Whose bells, the poor man's only music, rang
From morn to evening, all the hot Fair-day,
So sweetly, that they stirred and haunted me
With a wild pleasure, falling on mine ear
Most like articulate sounds of things to come!
So gazed I, till the soothing things, I dreamt,
Lulled me to sleep, and sleep prolonged my dreams!
And so I brooded all the following morn,
Awes by the stern preceptor's face, mine eye
Fixed with mock study on my swimming book:
Save if the door half opened, and I snatched
A hasty glance, and still my heart leaped up,
For still I hoped to see the *stranger*'s face,
Townsman, or aunt, or sister more beloved,
My play-mate when we both were clothed alike!

    Dear Babe, that sleepest cradled by my side,
Whose gentle breathings, heard in this deep calm,
Fill up the interspersèd vacancies

And momentary pauses of the thought!
My babe so beautiful it thrills my heart
With tender gladness, thus to look at thee,
And think that thou shalt learn far other lore,
And in far other scenes! For I was reared
In the great city, pent 'mid cloisters dim,
And saw nought lovely but the sky and stars.
But *thou*, my babe! shalt wander like a breeze
By lakes and sandy shores, beneath the crags
Of ancient mountain, and beneath the clouds,
Which image in their bulk both lakes and shores
And mountain crags: so shalt thou see and hear
The lovely shapes and sounds intelligible
Of that eternal language, which thy God
Utters, who from eternity doth teach
Himself in all, and all things in himself.
Great universal Teacher! he shall mould
Thy spirit, and by giving make it ask.

Therefore all seasons shall be sweet to thee,
Whether the summer clothe the general earth
With greenness, or the redbreast sit and sing
Betwixt the tufts of snow on the bare branch
Of mossy apple-tree, while the nigh thatch
Smokes in the sun-thaw; whether the eave-drops fall
Heard only in the trances of the blast,
Or if the secret ministry of frost
Shall hang them up in silent icicles,
Quietly shining to the quiet Moon.

Kubla Khan

In Xanadu did Kubla Khan
A stately pleasure-dome decree:
Where Alph, the sacred river, ran
Through caverns measureless to man
   Down to a sunless sea.
So twice five miles of fertile ground
With walls and towers were girdled round:

And there were gardens bright with sinuous rills,
Where blossomed many an incense-bearing tree;
And here were forests ancient as the hills,
Enfolding sunny spots of greenery.

But oh! that deep romantic chasm which slanted
Down the green hill athward a cedarn cover!
A savage place! as holy and enchanted
As e'er beneath a waning moon was haunted
By woman wailing for her demon-lover!
And from this chasm, with ceaseless turmoil seething,
As if this earth in fast thick pants were breathing,
A mighty fountain momently was forced:
Amid whose swift half-intermitted burst
Huge fragments vaulted like rebounding hail,
Or chaffy grain beneath the thresher's flail:
And 'mid these dancing rocks at once and ever
It flung up momently the sacred river.
Five miles meandering with a mazy motion
Through wood and dale the sacred river ran,
Then reached the caverns measureless to man,
And sank in tumult to a lifeless ocean:
And 'mid this tumult Kubla heard from far
Ancestral voices prophesying war!

    The shadow of the dome of pleasure
    Floated midway on the waves;
    Where was heard the mingled measure
    Form the fountain and the caves.
It was a miracle of rare device,
A sunny pleasure-dome with caves of ice!

    A damsel with a dulcimer
    In a vision once I saw:
    It was an Abyssinian maid,
    And on her dulcimer she played,
    Singing of Mount Abora.
    Could I revive within me
    Her symphony and song,
    To such a deep delight 'twould win me,
That with music loud and long,
I would build that dome in air,

That sunny dome! those caves of ice!
And all who heard should see them there,
And all should cry, Beware! Beware!
His flashing eyes, his floating hair!
Weave a circle round him thrice,
And close your eyes with holy dread,
For he on honey-dew hath fed,
And drunk the milk of Paradise.

PERCY BYSSHE SHELLEY

Ozymandias

I met a traveller from an antique land
Who said: Two vast and trunkless legs of stone
Stand in the desert... Near them, on the sand,
Half sunk, a shattered visage lies, whose frown,
And wrinkled lip, and sneer of cold command,
Tell that its sculptor well those passions read
Which yet survive, stamped on these lifeless things,
The hand that mocked them, and the heart that fed:
And on the pedestal these words appear:
'My name is Ozymandias, king of kings:
Look on my works, ye Mighty, and despair!'
Nothing beside remains. Round the decay
Of that colossal wreck, boundless and bare
The lone and level sands stretch far away.

Ode to the West Wind

I

O wild West Wind, thou breath of Autumn's being,
Thou, from whose unseen presence the leaves dead
Are driven, like ghosts from an enchanter fleeing,

Yellow, and black, and pale, and hectic red,
Pestilence-stricken multitudes: O thou,
Who chariotest to their dark wintry bed

The wingèd seeds, where they lie cold and low,
Each like a corpse within its grave, until
Thine azure sister of the Spring shall blow

Her clarion o'er the dreaming earth, and fill
(Driving sweet buds like flocks to feed in air)
With living hues and odours plain and hill:

Wild Spirit, which art moving everywhere;
Destroyer and preserver; hear, oh, hear!

II

Thou on whose stream, mid the steep sky's commotion,
Loose clouds like earth's decaying leaves are shed,
Shook from the tangled boughs of Heaven and Ocean,

Angels of rain and lightning: there are spread
On the blue surface of thine aëry surge,
Like the bright hair uplifted from the head

Of some fierce Maenad, even from the dim verge
Of the horizon to the zenith's height,
The locks of the approaching storm. Thou dirge

Of the dying year, to which this closing night
Will be the dome of a vast sepulchre,
Vaulted with all thy congregated might

Of vapours, from whose solid atmosphere
Black rain, and fire, and hail will burst: oh, hear!

III

Thou who didst waken from his summer dreams
The blue Mediterranean, where he lay,
Lulled by the coil of his crystàlline streams,

Beside a pumice isle in Baiae's bay,
And saw in sleep old palaces and towers
Quivering within the wave's intenser day,

All overgrown with azure moss, and flowers
So sweet, the sense faints picturing them! Thou
For whose path the Atlantic's level powers

Cleave themselves into chasms, while far below
The sea-blooms and the oozy woods which wear
The sapless foliage of the ocean, know

Thy voice, and suddenly grow gray with fear,
And tremble and despoil themselves: oh, hear!

IV

If I were a dead leaf thou mightest bear;
If I were a swift cloud to fly with thee;
A wave to pant beneath thy power, and share

The impulse of thy strength, only less free
Than thou, O uncontrollable! If even
I were as in my boyhood, and could be

The comrade of thy wanderings over Heaven,
As then, when to outstrip thy skiey speed
Scarces seemed a vision; I would ne'er have striven

As thus with thee in prayer in my sore need.
Oh, lift me as a wave, a leaf, a cloud!
I fall upon the thorns of life! I bleed!

A heavy weight of hours has chained and bowed
One too like thee: tameless, and swift, and proud.

V

Make me thy lyre, even as the forest is:
What if my leaves are falling like its own!
The tumult of thy mighty harmonies

Will take from both a deep, autumnal tone,
Sweet though in sadness. Be thou, Spirit fierce,
My spirit! Be thou me, impetuous one!

Drive my dead thoughts over the universe
Like withered leaves to quicken a new birth!
And, by the incantation of this verse,

Scatter, as from an unextinguished hearth
Ashes and sparks, my words among mankind!
Be through my lips to unawakened earth

The trumpet of a prophecy! O, Wind,
If Winter comes, can Spring be far behind?

JOHN KEATS

On First Looking into Chapman's Homer

Much have I travell'd in the realms of gold,
    And many goodly states and kingdoms seen;
    Round many western islands have I been
Which bards in fealty to Apollo hold.
Oft of one wide expanse had I been told
    That deep-brow'd Homer ruled as his demesne;
    Yet did I never breathe its pure serene
Till I heard Chapman speak out loud and bold:
Then felt I like some watcher of the skies
    When a new planet swims into his ken;
Or like stout Cortez when with eagle eyes
    He star'd at the Pacific – and all his men
Look'd at each other with a wild surmise –
    Silent, upon a peak in Darien.

Ode to a Nightingale

I

My heart aches, and a drowsy numbness pains
    My sense, as though of hemlock I had drunk,
Or emptied some dull opiate to the drains
    One minute past, and Lethe-wards had sunk:
'Tis not through envy of thy happy lot,
    But being too happy in thine happiness, –
        That thou, light-winged Dryad of the trees,
            In some melodious plot
    Of beechen green, and shadows numberless,
        Singest of summer in full-throated ease.

II

O, for a draught of vintage! that hath been
    Cool'd a long age in the deep-delved earth,
Tasting of Flora and the country green,
    Dance, and Provençal song, and sunburnt mirth!
O for a beaker full of the warm South,
    Full of the true, the blushful Hippocrene,
        With beaded bubbles winking at the brim,
            And purple-stained mouth;
    That I might drink, and leave the world unseen,
        And with thee fade away into the forest dim:

III

Fade far away, dissolve, and quite forget
    What thou among the leaves hast never known,
The weariness, the fever, and the fret
    Here, where men sit and hear each other groan;
Where palsy shakes a few, sad, last gray hairs,
    Where youth grows pale, and spectre-thin, and dies;
        Where but to think is to be full of sorrow
            And leaden-eyed despairs,
    Where Beauty cannot keep her lustrous eyes,
        Or new Love pine at them beyond to-morrow.

IV

Away! away! for I will fly to thee,
    Not charioted by Bacchus and his pards,
But on the viewless wings of Poesy,
    Though the dull brain perplexes and retards:
Already with thee! tender is the night,
    And haply the Queen-Moon is on her throne,
        Cluster'd around by all her starry Fays;
            But here there is no light,
    Save what from heaven is with the breezes blown
        Through verdurous glooms and winding mossy ways.

V

I cannot see what flowers are at my feet,
    Nor what soft incense hangs upon the boughs,
But, in embalmed darkness, guess each sweet
    Wherewith the seasonable month endows
The grass, the thicket, and the fruit-tree wild;
    White hawthorn, and the pastoral eglantine;
        Fast fading violets cover'd up in leaves;
            And mid-May's eldest child,
    The coming musk-rose, full of dewy wine,
        The murmurous haunt of flies on summer eves.

VI

Darkling I listen; and, for many a time
    I have been half in love with easeful Death,
Call'd him soft names in many a mused rhyme,
    To take into the air my quiet breath;
Now more than ever seems it rich to die,
    To cease upon the midnight with no pain,
        While thou art pouring forth thy soul abroad
            In such an ecstasy!
    Still wouldst thou sing, and I have ears in vain –
        To thy high requiem become a sod.

VII

Thou wast not born for death, immortal Bird!
    No hungry generations tread thee down;
The voice I hear this passing night was heard
    In ancient days by emperor and clown:
Perhaps the self-same song that found a path
        Through the sad heart of Ruth, when, sick for home,
            She stood in tears amid the alien corn;
                The same that oft-times hath
        Charm'd magic casements, opening on the foam
    Of perilous seas, in faery lands forlorn.

VIII

Forlorn! the very word is like a bell
    To toll me back from thee to my sole self!
Adieu! the fancy cannot cheat so well
    As she is fam'd to do, deceiving elf.
Adieu! adieu! thy plaintive anthem fades
        Past the near meadows, over the still stream,
            Up the hill-side; and now 'tis buried deep
                In the next valley-glades:
        Was it a vision, or a waking dream?
        Fled is that music: – Do I wake or sleep?

Ode on a Grecian Urn

I

Thou still unravish'd bride of quietness,
    Thou foster-child of silence and slow time,
Sylvan historian, who canst thus express
    A flowery tale more sweetly than our rhyme:
What leaf-fring'd legend haunts about thy shape
    Of deities or mortals, or of both,
        In Tempe or the dales of Arcady?
    What men or gods are these? What maidens loth?
What mad pursuit? What struggle to escape?
        What pipes and timbrels? What wild ecstasy?

II

Heard melodies are sweet, but those unheard
    Are sweeter; therefore, ye soft pipes, play on;
Not to the sensual ear, but, more endear'd,
    Pipe to the spirit ditties of no tone:
Fair youth, beneath the trees, thou canst not leave
    Thy song, nor ever can those trees be bare;
        Bold Lover, never, never canst thou kiss,
Though winning near the goal – yet, do not grieve;
    She cannot fade, though thou hast not thy bliss,
        For ever wilt thou love, and she be fair!

III

Ah, happy, happy boughs! that cannot shed
    Your leaves, nor ever bid the Spring adieu;
And, happy melodist, unwearied,
    For ever piping songs for ever new;
More happy love! more happy, happy love!
    For ever warm and still to be enjoy'd,
        For ever panting, and for ever young;
All breathing human passion far above,
    That leaves a heart high-sorrowful and cloy'd,
        A burning forehead, and a parching tongue.

IV

Who are these coming to the sacrifice?
    To what green altar, O mysterious priest,
Lead'st thou that heifer lowing at the skies,
    And all her silken flanks with garlands drest?
What little town by river or sea shore,
    Or mountain-built with peaceful citadel,
        Is emptied of this folk, this pious morn?
And, little town, thy streets for evermore
    Will silent be; and not a soul to tell
        Why thou art desolate, can e'er return.

V

O Attic shape! Fair attitude! with brede
   Of marble men and maidens overwrought,
With forest branches and the trodden weed;
   Thou, silent form, dost tease us out of thought
As doth eternity: Cold Pastoral!
   When old age shall this generation waste,
     Thou shalt remain, in midst of other woe
Than ours, a friend to man, to whom thou say'st,
   'Beauty is truth, truth beauty,' – that is all
     Ye know on earth, and all ye need to know.

Ode to Psyche

O Goddess! hear these tuneless numbers, wrung
   By sweet enforcement and remembrance dear,
And pardon that thy secrets should be sung
   Even into thine own soft-conched ear:
Surely I dreamt to-day, or did I see
   The winged Psyche with awaken'd eyes?
I wander'd in a forest thoughtlessly,
   And, on the sudden, fainting with surprise,
Saw two fair creatures, couched side by side
   In deepest grass, beneath the whisp'ring roof
   Of leaves and trembled blossoms, where there ran
     A brooklet, scarce espied:

'Mid hush'd, cool-rooted flowers, fragrant-eyed,
   Blue, silver-white, and budded Tyrian,
They lay calm-breathing on the bedded grass;
   Their arms embraced, and their pinions too;
   Their lips touch'd not, but had not bade adieu,
As if disjoined by soft-handed slumber,
And ready still past kisses to outnumber
   At tender eye-dawn of aurorean lore:
     The winged boy I knew;
   But who wast thou, O happy, happy dove?
     His Psyche true!

O latest born and loveliest vision far
 Of all Olympus' faded hierarchy!
Fairer than Phœbe's sapphire-region'd star,
 Or Vesper, amorous glow-worm of the sky;
Fairer than these, though temple thou hast none,
  Nor altar heap'd with flowers;
Nor virgin-choir to make delicious moan
  Upon the midnight hours;
No voice, no lute, no pipe, no incense sweet
 From chain-swung censer teeming;
No shrine, no grove, no oracle, no heat
 Of pale-mouth'd prophet dreaming.

O brightest! though too late for antique vows,
 Too, too late for the fond believing lyre,
When holy were the haunted forest boughs,
 Holy the air, the water, and the fire:
Yet even in these days so far retir'd
 From happy pieties, thy lucent fans,
 Fluttering among the faint Olympians,
I see, and sing, by my own eyes inspir'd.
So let me be thy choir, and make a moan
  Upon the midnight hours;
Thy voice, thy lute, thy pipe, thy incense sweet
 From swinged censer teeming;
Thy shrine, thy grove, thy oracle, thy heat
 Of pale-mouth'd prophet dreaming.

Yes, I will be thy priest, and build a fane
 In some untrodden region of my mind,
Where branched thoughts, new grown with pleasant pain,
 Instead of pines shall murmur in the wind:
Far, far around shall those dark-cluster'd trees
 Fledge the wild-ridged mountains steep by steep;
And there by zephyrs, streams, and birds, and bees,
 The moss-lain Dryads shall be lull'd to sleep;
And in the midst of this wide quietness
A rosy sanctuary will I dress
With the wreath'd trellis of a working brain,
 With buds, and bells, and stars without a name,
With all the gardener Fancy e'er could feign,
 Who breeding flowers, will never breed the same:

And there shall be for thee all soft delight
   That shadowy thought can win,
A bright torch, and a casement ope at night,
   To let the warm Love in!

Sonnet

ON THE SEA

It keeps eternal whisperings around
   Desolate shores, and with its mighty swell
   Gluts twice ten thousand Caverns, till the spell
Of Hecate leaves them their old shadowy sound.
Often 'tis in such gentle temper found,
   That scarcely will the very smallest shell
   Be mov'd for days from where it sometime fell,
When last the winds of Heaven were unbound.
Oh ye! who have your eye-balls vex'd and tir'd,
   Feast them upon the wideness of the Sea;
     Oh ye! whose ears are dinn'd with uproar rude,
     Or fed too much with cloying melody –
     Sit ye near some old Cavern's Mouth, and brood
Until ye start, as if the sea-nymphs quir'd!

Sonnet

When I have fears that I may cease to be
   Before my pen has glean'd my teeming brain,
Before high-piled books, in charactery,
   Hold like rich garners the full ripen'd grain;
When I behold, upon the night's starr'd face,
   Huge cloudy symbols of a high romance,
And think that I may never live to trace
   Their shadows, with the magic hand of chance;
And when I feel, fair creature of an hour,
   That I shall never look upon thee more,

Never have relish in the faery power
     Of unreflecting love; – then on the shore
Of the wide world I stand alone, and think
Till love and fame to nothingness do sink.

La Belle Dame Sans Merci

I

Ah, what can ail thee, wretched wight,
     Alone and palely loitering;
The sedge is wither'd from the lake,
     And no birds sing.

II

Ah, what can ail thee, wretched wight,
     So haggard and so woe-begone?
The squirrel's granary is full,
     And the harvest's done.

III

I see a lilly on thy brow,
     With anguish moist and fever dew;
And on thy cheek a fading rose
     Fast withereth too.

IV

I met a lady in the meads
     Full beautiful, a faery's child;
Her hair was long, her foot was light,
     And her eyes were wild.

V

I set her on my pacing steed,
     And nothing else saw all day long;
For sideways would she lean, and sing
     A faery's song.

VI

I made a garland for her head,
    And bracelets too, and fragrant zone;
She look'd at me as she did love,
    And made sweet moan.

VII

She found me roots of relish sweet,
    And honey wild, and manna dew;
And sure in language strange she said,
    I love thee true.

VIII

She took me to her elfin grot,
    And there she gaz'd and sighed deep,
And there I shut her wild sad eyes –
    So kiss'd to sleep.

IX

And there we slumber'd on the moss,
    And there I dream'd, ah woe betide,
The latest dream I ever dream'd
    On the cold hill side.

X

I saw pale kings, and princes too,
    Pale warriors, death-pale were they all;
Why cry'd – 'La belle Dame sans merci
    Hath thee in thrall!'

XI

I saw their starv'd lips in the gloam
    With horrid warning gaped wide,
And I awoke, and found me here
    On the cold hill side.

XII

And this is why I sojourn here
    Alone and palely loitering,
Though the sedge is wither'd from the lake,
    And no birds sing.

ALFRED, LORD TENNYSON

Ulysses

It little profits that an idle king,
By this still hearth, among these barren crags,
Match'd with an aged wife, I mete and dole
Unequal laws unto a savage race,
That hoard, and sleep, and feed, and know not me.
I cannot rest from travel; I will drink
Life to the lees. All times I have enjoy'd
Greatly, have suffer'd greatly, both with those
That loved me, and alone; on shore, and when
Thro' scudding drifts the rainy Hyades
Vext the dim sea. I am become a name;
For always roaming with a hungry heart
Much have I seen and known, – cities of men
And manners, climates, councils, governments,
Myself not least, but honor'd of them all, –
And drunk delight of battle with my peers,
Far on the ringing plains of windy Troy.
I am a part of all that I have met;
Yet all experience is an arch wherethro'
Gleams that untravell'd world whose margin fades
For ever and for ever when I move.
How dull it is to pause, to make an end,
To rest unburnish'd, not to shine in use!
As tho' to breathe were life! Life piled on life
Were all too little, and of one to me
Little remains; but every hour is saved
From that eternal silence, something more,
A bringer of new things; and vile it were
For some three suns to store and hoard myself,
And this gray spirit yearning in desire
To follow knowledge like a sinking star,
Beyond the utmost bound of human thought.
   This is my son, mine own Telemachus,
To whom I leave the sceptre and the isle, –
Well-loved of me, discerning to fulfil
This labor, by slow prudence to make mild
A rugged people, and thro' soft degrees

Subdue them to the useful and the good.
Most blameless is he, centred in the sphere
Of common duties, decent not to fail
In offices of tenderness, and pay
Meet adoration to my household gods,
When I am gone. He works his work, I mine.
  There lies the port; the vessel puffs her sail;
There gloom the dark, broad seas. My mariners,
Souls that have toil'd, and wrought, and thought with me, –
That ever with a frolic welcome took
The thunder and the sunshine, and opposed
Free hearts, free foreheads, – you and I are old;
Old age hath yet his honor and his toil.
Death closes all; but something ere the end,
Some work of noble note, may yet be done,
Not unbecoming men that strove with Gods.
The lights begin to twinkle from the rocks;
The long day wanes; the slow moon climbs; the deep
Moans round with many voices. Come, my friends.
'T is not too late to seek a newer world.
Push off, and sitting well in order smite
The sounding furrows; for my purpose holds
To sail beyond the sunset, and the baths
Of all the western stars, until I die.
It may be that the gulfs will wash us down;
It may be we shall touch the Happy isles,
And see the great Achilles, whom we knew.
Tho' much is taken, much abides; and tho'
We are not now that strength which in old days
Moved earth and heaven, that which we are, we are, –
One equal temper of heroic hearts,
Made weak by time and fate, but strong in will
To strive, to seek, to find, and not to yield.

The Charge of the Light Brigade

I

Half a league, half a league,
Half a league onward,
All in the valley of Death
    Rode the six hundred.
'Forward the Light Brigade!
Charge for the guns!' he said.
Into the valley of Death
    Rode the six hundred.

II

'Forward, the Light Brigade!'
Was there a man dismay'd?
Not tho' the soldier knew
    Some one had blunder'd.
Theirs not to make reply,
Theirs not to reason why,
Theirs but to do and die.
Into the valley of Death
    Rode the six hundred.

III

Cannon to right of them,
Cannon to left of them,
Cannon in front of them
    Volley'd and thunder'd;
Storm'd at with shot and shell,
Boldly they rode and well,
Into the jaws of Death,
Into the mouth of hell
    Rode the six hundred.

IV

Flash'd all their sabres bare,
Flash'd as they turn'd in air
Sabring the gunners there,
Charging an army, while
    All the world wonder'd.

Plunged in the battery-smoke
Right thro' the line they broke;
Cossack and Russian
Reel'd from the sabre-stroke
    Shatter'd and sunder'd.
Then they rode back, but not,
    Not the six hundred.

V

Cannon to right of them,
Cannon to left of them,
Cannon behind them
    Volley'd and thunder'd;
Storm'd at with shot and shell,
While horse and hero fell,
They that had fought so well
Came thro' the jaws of Death,
Back from the mouth of hell,
All that was left of them,
    Left of six hundred.

VI

When can their glory fade?
O the wild charge they made!
    All the world wonder'd.
Honor the charge they made!
Honor the Light Brigade,
    Noble six hundred!

ROBERT BROWNING

My Last Duchess

FERRARA

That's my last Duchess painted on the wall,
Looking as if the were alive. I call
That piece a wonder, now: Frà Pandolf's hands
Worked busily a day, and there she stands.
Will 't please you sit and look at her? I said
'Frà Pandolf' by design: for never read
Strangers like you that pictured countenance,
The depth and passion of its earnest glance,
But to myself they turned (since none puts by
The curtain I have drawn for you, but I)
And seemed as they would ask me, if they durst,
How such a glance came there; so, not the first
Are you to turn and ask thus. Sir, 't was not
Her husband's presence only, called that spot
Of joy into the Duchess' cheek: perhaps
Frà Pandolf chanced to say 'Her mantle laps
Over my lady's wrist too much,' or 'Paint
Must never hope to reproduce the faint
Half-flush that dies along her throat:' such stuff
Was courtesy, she thought, and cause enough
For calling up that spot of joy. She had
A heart – how shall I say? – too soon made glad,
Too easily impressed; the liked whate'er
She looked on, and her looks went everywhere.
Sir, 't was all one! My favour at her breast,
The dropping of the daylight in the West,
The bough of cherries some officious fool
Broke in the orchard for her, the white mule
She rode with round the terrace – all and each
Would draw from her alike the approving speech,
Or blush, at least. She thanked men, – good! but thanked
Somehow – I know not how – as if she ranked
My gift of a nine-hundred-years-old name
With anybody's gift. Who'd stoop to blame
This sort of trifling? Even had you skill

In speech – (which I have not) – to make your will
Quite clear to such an one, and say, 'Just this
Or that in you disgusts me; here you miss,
Or there exceed the mark' – and if she let
Herself be lessoned so, nor plainly set
Her wits to yours, forsooth, and made excuse,
– E'en then would be some stooping; and I choose
Never to stop. Oh sir, she smiled, no doubt,
Whene'er I passed her; but who passed without
Much the same smile? This grew; I gave commands;
Then all smiles stopped together. There she stands
As if alive. Will 't please you rise? We'll meet
The company below, then. I repeat,
The Count your master's known munificence
Is ample warrant that no just pretence
Of mine for dowry will be disallowed;
Though his fair daughter's self, as I avowed
At starting, is my object. Nay, we'll go
Together down, sir. Notice Neptune, though,
Taming a sea-horse, thought a rarity,
Which Claus of Innsbruck cast in bronze for me!

Home-Thoughts from Abroad

I

Oh, to be in England now that April's there,
And whoever wakes in England sees, some morning, unaware,
That the lowest boughs and the brushwood sheaf
Round the elm-tree bole are in tiny leaf,
While the chaffinch sings on the orchard bough
In England – now!

II

And after April, when May follows
And the white-throat builds, and all the swallows!
Hark, where my blossomed pear-tree in the hedge
Leans to the field and scatters on the clover

Blossoms and dewdrops – at the bent spray's edge –
That's the wise thrush: he sings each song twice over
Lest you should think he never could recapture
The first fine careless rapture!
And, tho' the fields look rough with hoary dew,
All will be gay when noontide wakes anew
The buttercups, the little children's dower
– Far brighter than this gaudy melon-flower!

Meeting at Night

I

The gray sea and the long black land;
And the yellow half-moon large and low;
And the startled little waves that leap
In fiery ringlets from their sleep,
As I gain the cove with pushing prow,
And quench its speed i' the slushy sand.

II

Then a mile of warm sea-scented beach;
Three fields to cross till a farm appears;
A tap at the pane, the quick sharp scratch
And blue spurt of a lighted match,
And a voice less loud, thro' its joys and fears,
Than the two hearts beating each to each!

Andrea del Sarto

(CALLED 'THE FAULTLESS PAINTER')

But do not let us quarrel any more,
No, my Lucrezia! bear with me for once:
Sit down and all shall happen as you wish.
You turn your face, but does it bring your heart?

I'll work then for your friend's friend, never fear,
Treat his own subject after his own way,
Fix his own time, accept too his own price,
And shut the money into this small hand
When next it takes mine. Will it? tenderly?
Oh, I'll content him, – but to-morrow, Love!
I often am much wearier than you think,
This evening more than usual: and it seems
As if – forgive now – should you let me sit
Here by the window, with your hand in mine,
And look a half-hour forth on Fiesole,
Both of one mind, as married people use,
Quietly, quietly the evening through,
I might get up to-morrow to my work
Cheerful and fresh as ever. Let us try.
To-morrow, how you shall be glad for this!
Your soft hand is a woman of itself,
And mine the man's bared breast she curls inside.
Don't count the time lost, neither; you must serve
For each of the five pictures we require:
It saves a model. So! keep looking so –
My serpentining beauty, rounds on rounds!
– How could you ever prick those perfect ears,
Even to put the pearl there! oh, so sweet –
My face, my moon, my everybody's moon,
Which everybody looks on and calls his,
And, I suppose, is looked on by in turn,
While she looks – no one's: very dear, no less.
You smile? why, there's my picture ready made,
There's what we painters call our harmony!
A common grayness silvers everything, –
All in a twilight, you and I alike
– You, at the point of your first pride in me
(That's gone, you know) – but I, at every point;
My youth, my hope, my art, being all toned down
To yonder sober pleasant Fiesole.
There's the bell clinking from the chapel-top;
That length of convent-wall across the way
Holds the trees safer, huddled more inside;
The last monk leaves the garden; days decrease,
And autumn grows, autumn in everything.
Eh? the whole seems to fall into a shape,

129

As if I saw alike my work and self
And all that I was born to be and do,
A twilight-piece. Love, we are in God's hand.
How strange now, looks the life he makes us lead;
So free we seem, so fettered fast we are!
I feel he laid the fetter: let it lie!
This chamber for example – turn your head –
All that's behind us! You don't understand
Nor care to understand about my art,
But you can hear at least when people speak:
And that cartoon, the second from the door
– It is the thing, Love! so such things should be –
Behold Madonna! – I am bold to say.
I can do with my pencil what I know,
What I see, what at bottom of my heart
I wish for, if I ever wish so deep –
Do easily, too – when I say, perfectly,
I do not boast, perhaps: yourself are judge,
Who listened to the Legate's talk last week;
And just as much they used to say in France.
At any rate 't is easy, all of it!
No sketches first, no studies, that's long past:
I do what many dream of, all their lives,
– Dream? strive to do, and agonize to do,
And fail in doing. I could count twenty such
On twice your fingers, and not leave this town,
Who strive – you don't know how the others strive
To paint a little thing like that you smeared
Carelessly passing with your robes afloat, –
Yet do much less, so much less, Someone says,
(I know his name, no matter) – so much less!
Well, less is more, Lucrezia: I am judged.
There burns a truer light of God in them,
In their vexed beating stuffed and stopped-up brain,
Heart, or whate'er else, than goes on to prompt
This low-pulsed forthright craftsman's hand of mine.
Their works drop groundward, but themselves, I know,
Reach many a time a heaven that's shut to me,
Enter and take their place there sure enough,
Tho' they come back and cannot tell the world.
My works are nearer heaven, but I sit here.
The sudden blood of these men! at a word –

Praise them, it boils, or blames them, it boils too.
I, painting from myself and to myself,
Know what I do, am unmoved by men's blame
Or their praise either. Somebody remarks
Morello's outline there is wrongly traced,
His hue mistaken; what of that? or else,
Rightly traced and well ordered; what of that?
Speak as they please, what does the mountain care?
Ah, but a man's reach should exceed his grasp,
Or what's a heaven for? All is silver-gray,
Placid and perfect with my art: the worse!
I know both what I want and what might gain,
And yet how profitless to know, to sigh
'Had I been two, another and myself,
Our head would have o'erlooked the world!' No doubt.
Yonder's a work now, of that famous youth
The Urbinate who died five years ago.
('T is copied, George Vasari sent it me.)
Well, I can fancy how he did it all,
Pouring his soul, with kings and popes to see,
Reaching, that heaven might so replenish him,
Above and thro' his art – for it gives way;
That arm is wrongly put – and there again –
A fault to pardon in the drawing's lines,
Its body, so to speak: its soul is right,
He means right – that, a child may understand.
Still, what an arm! and I could alter it:
But all the play, the insight and the stretch –
Out of me, out of me! And wherefore out?
Had you enjoined them on me, given me soul,
We might have risen to Rafael, I and you!
Nay, Love, you did give all I asked, I think –
More than I merit, yes, by many times.
But had you – oh, with the same perfect brow,
And perfect eyes, and more than perfect mouth,
And the low voice my soul hears, as a bird
The fowler's pipe, and follows to the snare –
Had you, with these the same, but brought a mind!
Some women do so. Had the mouth there urged
'God and the glory! never care for gain.
The present by the future, what is that?
Live for fame, side by side with Agnolo!

Rafael is waiting: up to God, all three!'
I might have done it for you. So it seems:
Perhaps not. All is as God over-rules.
Beside, incentives come from the soul's self;
The rest avail not. Why do I need you?
What wife had Rafael, or has Agnolo?
In this world, who can do a thing, will not;
And who would do it, can not, I perceive:
Yet the will's somewhat – somewhat, too, the power
And thus we half-men struggle. At the end,
God, I conclude, compensates, punishes.
'T is safer for me, if the award be strict,
That I am something underrated here,
Poor this long while, despised, to speak the truth.
I dared not, do you know, leave home all day,
For fear of chancing on the Paris lords.
The best is when they pass and look aside;
But they speak sometimes; I must bear it all.
Well may they speak! That Francis, that first time,
And that long festal year at Fontainebleau!
I surely then could sometimes leave the ground,
Put on the glory, Rafael's daily wear,
In that humane great monarch's golden look, –
One finger in his beard or twisted curl
Over his mouth's good mark that made the smile,
One arm about my shoulder, round my neck,
The jingle of his gold chain in my ear,
I painting proudly with his breath on me,
All his court round him, seeing with his eyes,
Such frank French eyes, and such a fire of souls
Profuse, my hand kept plying by those hearts, –
And, best of all, this, this, this face beyond,
This in the background, waiting on my work,
To crown the issue with a last reward!
A good time, was it not, my kingly days?
And had you not grown restless...but I know –
'T is done and past; 't was right, my instinct said;
Too live the life grew, golden and not gray:
And I'm the weak-eyed bat no sun should tempt
Out of the grange whose four walls make his world.
How could it end in any other way?
You called me, and I came home to your heart.

The triumph was – to reach and stay there; since
I reached it ere the triumph, what is lost?
Let my hands frame your face in your hair's gold,
You beautiful Lucrezia that are mine!
'Rafael did this, Andrea painted that;
The Roman's is the better when you pray,
But still the other's Virgin was his wife –'
Men will excuse me. I am glad to judge
Both pictures in your presence; clearer grows
My better fortune, I resolve to think.
For, do you know, Lucrezia, as God lives,
Said one day Agnolo, his very self,
To Rafael... I have known it all these years...
(When the young man was flaming out his thoughts
Upon a palace-wall for Rome to see,
Too lifted up in heart because of it)
'Friend, there's a certain sorry little scrub
Goes up and down our Florence, none cares how,
Who, were he set to plan and execute
As you are, pricked on by your popes and kings,
Would bring the sweat into that brow of yours!'
To Rafael's! – And indeed the arm is wrong.
I hardly dare... yet, only you to see,
Give the chalk here – quick, thus the line should go!
Ay, but the soul! he's Rafael! rub it out!
Still, all I care for, if he spoke the truth,
(What he? why, who but Michel Agnolo?
Do you forget already words like those?)
If really there was such a chance so lost, –
Is, whether you're – not grateful – but more pleased.
Well, let me think so. And you smile indeed!
This hour has been an hour? Another smile?
If you would sit thus by me every night
I should work better, do you comprehend?
I mean that I should earn more, give you more.
See, it is settled dusk now; there's a star;
Morello's gone, the watch-lights show the wall,
The cue-owls speak the name we call them by.
Come from the window, love, – come in, at last,
Inside the melancholy little house
We built to be so gay with. God is just.
King Francis may forgive me: oft at nights

When I look up from painting, eyes tired out,
The walls become illumined, brick from brick
Distinct, instead of mortar, fierce bright gold,
That gold of his I did cement them with!
Let us but love each other. Must you go?
That Cousin here again? he waits outside?
Must see you – you, and not with me? Those loans?
More gaming debts to pay? you smiled for that?
Well, let smiles buy me! have you more to spend?
While hand and eye and something of a heart
Are left me, work's my ware, and what's it worth?
I'll pay my fancy. Only let me sit
The gray remainder of the evening out,
Idle, you call it, and muse perfectly
How I could paint, were I but back in France,
One picture, just one more – the Virgin's face,
Not yours this time! I want you at my side
To hear them – that is, Michel Agnolo –
Judge all I do and tell you of its worth.
Will you? To-morrow, satisfy your friend.
I take the subjects for his corridor,
Finish the portrait out of hand – there, there,
And throw him in another thing or two
If he demurs; the whole should prove enough
To pay for this same Cousin's freak. Beside,
What's better and what's all I care about,
Get you the thirteen scudi for the ruff!
Love, does that please you? Ah, but what does he,
The Cousin! what does he to please you more?

    I am grown peaceful as old age to-night.
I regret little, I would change still less.
Since there my past life lies, why alter it?
The very wrong to Francis! – it is true
I took his coin, was tempted and complied,
And built this house and sinned, and all is said.
My father and my mother died of want.
Well, had I riches of my own? you see
How one gets rich! Let each one bear his lot.
They were born poor, lived poor, and poor they died:
And I have laboured somewhat in my time
And not been paid profusely. Some good son
Paint my two hundred pictures – let him try!

No doubt, there's something strikes a balance. Yes,
You loved me quite enough, it seems to-night.
This must suffice me here. What would one have?
In heaven, perhaps, new chances, one more chance –
Four great walls in the New Jerusalem,
Meted on each side by the angel's reed,
For Leonard, Rafael, Agnolo and me
To cover – the three first without a wife,
While I have mine! So – still they overcome
Because there's still Lucrezia, – as I choose.

Again the Cousin's whistle! Go, my Love.

Two in the Campagna

I

I wonder do you feel to-day
  As I have felt since, hand in hand,
We sat down on the grass, to stray
  In spirit better thro' the land,
This morn of Rome and May?

II

For me, I touched a thought, I know,
  Has tantalized me many times,
(Like turns of thread the spiders throw
  Mocking across our path) for rhymes
To catch at and let go.

III

Help me to hold it! First it left
  The yellowing fennel, run to seed
There, branching from the brickwork's cleft,
  Some old tomb's ruin: yonder weed
Took up the floating weft,

IV

Where one small orange cup amassed
   Five beetles, – blind and green they grope
Among the honey-meal: and last,
   Everywhere on the grassy slope,
I traced it. Hold it fast!

V

The champaign with its endless fleece
   Of feathery grasses everywhere!
Silence and passion, joy and peace,
   An everlasting wash of air –
Rome's ghost since her decease.

VI

Such life here, thro' such lengths of hours,
   Such miracles performed in play,
Such primal naked forms of flowers,
   Such letting nature have her way
While heaven looks from its towers!

VII

How say you? Let us, O my dove,
   Let us be unashamed of soul,
As earth lies bare to heaven above!
   How is it under our control
To love or not to love?

VIII

I would that you were all to me,
   You that are just so much, no more.
Nor yours nor mine, nor slave nor free!
   Where does the fault lie? What the core
O' the wound, since wound must be?

IX

I would I could adopt your will,
   See with your eyes, and set my heart

Beating by yours, and drink my fill
    At your soul's springs, – your part my part
In life, for good and ill.

X

No, I yearn upward, touch you close,
    Then stand away. I kiss your cheek,
Catch your soul's warmth, – I pluck the rose
    And love it more than tongue can speak –
Then the good minute goes.

XI

Already how am I so far
    Out of that minute? Must I go
Still like the thistle-ball, no bar,
    Onward, whenever light winds blow,
Fixed by no friendly star?

XII

Just when I seemed about to learn!
    Where is the thread now? Off again.
The old trick! Only I discern –
    Infinite passion, and the pain
Of finite hearts that yearn.

ARTHUR HUGH CLOUGH

from *Amours de Voyage*

Canto III

Yet to the wondrous St. Peter's, and yet to the solemn Rotonda,
    Mingling with heroes and gods, yet to the Vatican Walls,
Yet may we go, and recline, while a whole mighty world seems above us,
    Gathered and fixed to all time into one roofing supreme;
Yet may we, thinking on these things, exclude what is meaner around us;

Yet, at the worst of the worst, books and a chamber remain;
Yet may we think, and forget, and possess our souls in resistance. –
   Ah, but away from the stir, shouting, and gossip of war,
Where, upon Apennine slope, with the chestnut the oak-trees immingle,
   Where, amid odorous copse bridle-paths wander and wind,
Where, under mulberry-branches, the diligent rivulet sparkles,
   Or amid cotton and maize peasants their water-works ply,
Where, over fig-tree and orange in tier upon tier still repeated,
   Garden on garden upreared, balconies step to the sky, –
Ah, that I were far away from the crowd and the streets of the city,
   Under the vine-trellis laid, O my beloved, with thee!

III   CLAUDE TO EUSTACE

Farewell, Politics, utterly! What can I do? I cannot
Fight, you know; and to talk I am wholly ashamed. And although I
Gnash my teeth when I look in your French or your English papers,
What is the good of that? Will swearing, I wonder, mend matters?
Cursing and scolding repel the assailants? No, it is idle;
No, whatever befalls, I will hide, will ignore or forget it.
Let the tail shift for itself; I will bury my head. And what's the
Roman Republic to me, or I to the Roman Republic?

   Why not fight? – In the first place, I haven't so much as a musket;
In the next, if I had, I shouldn't know how I should use it;
In the third, just at present I'm studying ancient marbles;
In the fourth, I consider I owe my life to my country;
In the fifth – I forget, but four good reasons are ample.
Meantime, pray let 'em fight, and be killed. I delight in devotion.
So that I 'list not, hurrah for the glorious army of martyrs!
Sanguis martyrum semen Ecclesiæ; though it would seem this
Church is indeed of the purely Invisible Kingdom-come kind:
Militant here on earth! Triumphant, of course, then, elsewhere!
Ah, good Heaven, but I would I were out far away from the pother!

IV   CLAUDE TO EUSTACE

Not, as we read in the words of the olden-time inspiration,
Are there two several trees in the place we are set to abide in;
But on the apex most high of the Tree of Life in the Garden,
Budding, unfolding, and falling, decaying and flowering ever,
Flowering is set and decaying the transient blossom of Knowledge, –

Flowering alone, and decaying, the needless unfruitful blossom.
Or as the cypress-spires by the fair-flowing stream Hellespontine,
Which from the mythical tomb of the godlike Protesilaüs
Rose sympathetic in grief to his love-lorn Laodamia,
Evermore growing, and, when in their growth to the prospect attaining,
Over the low sea-banks, of the fatal Ilian city,
Withering still at the sight which still they upgrow to encounter.
Ah, but ye that extrude from the ocean your helpless faces,
Ye over stormy seas leading long and dreary processions,
Ye, too, brood of the wind, whose coming is whence we discern not,
Making your nest on the wave, and your bed on the crested billow,
Skimming rough waters, and crowding wet sands that the tide shall
    return to,
Cormorants, ducks, and gulls, fill ye my imagination!
Let us not talk of growth; we are still in our Aqueous Ages.

XI   CLAUDE TO EUSTACE

Tibur is beautiful, too, and the orchard slopes, and the Anio
Falling, falling yet, to the ancient lyrical cadence;
Tibur and Anio's tide; and cool from Lucretilis ever,
With the Digentian stream, and with the Bandusian fountain,
Folded in Sabine recesses, the valley and villa of Horace: –
So not seeing I sang; so seeing and listening say I,
Here as I sit by the stream, as I gaze at the cell of the Sibyl,
Here with Albunea's home and the grove of Tiburnus beside me;[1]
Tivoli beautiful is, and musical, O Teverone,
Dashing from mountain to plain, thy parted impetuous waters!
Tivoli's waters and rocks; and fair unto Monte Gennaro
(Haunt even yet, I must think, as I wander and gaze, of the shadows,
Faded and pale, yet immortal, of Faunus, the Nymphs, and the Graces),
Fair in itself, and yet fairer with human completing creations,
Folded in Sabine recesses the valley and villa of Horace: –
So not seeing I sang; so now – Nor seeing, nor hearing,
Neither by waterfall lulled, nor folded in sylvan embraces,
Neither by cell of the Sibyl, nor stepping the Monte Gennaro,
Seated on Anio's bank, nor sipping Bandusian waters,
But on Montorio's height, looking down on the tile-clad streets, the
Cupolas, crosses, and domes, the bushes and kitchen-gardens,

[1]   – domus Albuneæ resonantis, / Et præceps Anio, et Tiburni lucus, et uda / Mobilibus
    pomaria rivis.

Which, by the grace of the Tiber, proclaim themselves Rome of the
      Romans, –
But on Montorio's height, looking forth to the vapoury mountains,
Cheating the prisoner Hope with illusions of vision and fancy, –
But on Montorio's height, with these weary soldiers by me,
Waiting till Oudinot enter, to reinstate Pope and Tourist.

MATTHEW ARNOLD

Shakespeare

Others abide our question. Thou art free.
We ask and ask: Thou smilest and art still,
Out-topping knowledge. For the loftiest hill
That to the stars uncrowns his majesty,
Planting his stedfast footsteps in the sea,
Making the Heaven of Heavens his dwelling-place,
Spares but the cloudy border of his base
To the foil'd searching of mortality:
And thou, who didst the stars and sunbeams know,
Self-school'd, self-scann'd, self-honour'd, self-secure,
Didst walk on Earth unguess'd at. Better so!
All pains the immortal spirit must endure,
All weakness that impairs, all griefs that bow,
Find their sole voice in that victorious brow.

The Scholar Gipsy

There was very lately a lad in the University of Oxford who was by his
poverty forced to leave his studies there; and at last to join himself to a
company of vagabond gipsies. Among these extravagant people, by the
insinuating subtilty of his carriage, he quickly got so much of their love and
esteem as that they discovered to him their mystery. After he had been a
pretty while well exercised in the trade, there chanced to ride by a couple
of scholars, who had formerly been of his acquaintance. They quickly spied
out their old friend among the gipsies; and he gave them an account of the
necessity which drove him to that kind of life, and told them that the
people he went with were not such impostors as they were taken for, but
that they had a traditional kind of learning among them, and could do
wonders by the power of imagination, their fancy binding that of others:
that himself had learned much of their art, and when he had compassed the
whole secret, he intended, he said, to leave their company, and give the
world an account of what he had learned.

– GLANVIL's *Vanity of Dogmatizing*, 1661.

Go, for they call you, Shepherd, from the hill;
   Go, Shepherd, and untie the wattled cotes:
     No longer leave thy wistful flock unfed,
   Nor let thy bawling fellows rack their throats,
     Nor the cropp'd grasses shoot another head.
       But when the fields are still,
   And the tired men and dogs all gone to rest,
     And only the white sheep are sometimes seen
     Cross and recross the strips of moon-blanch'd green;
      Come, Shepherd, and again renew the quest.

Here, where the reaper was at work of late,
   In this high field's dark corner, where he leaves
     His coat, his basket, and his earthen cruise,
   And in the sun all morning binds the sheaves,
     Then here, at noon, comes back his stores to use;
       Here will I sit and wait,
   While to my ear from uplands far away
     The bleating of the folded flocks is borne,
     With distant cries of reapers in the corn –
      All the live murmur of a summer's day.

Screen'd is this nook o'er the high, half-reap'd field,
   And here till sun-down, Shepherd, will I be.
     Through the thick corn the scarlet poppies peep

And round green roots and yellowing stalks I see
　　Pale blue convolvulus in tendrils creep:
　　　　And air-swept lindens yield
Their scent, and rustle down their perfum'd showers
　　Of bloom on the bent grass where I am laid,
　　　　And bower me from the August sun with shade;
　　　　And the eye travels down to Oxford's towers:

And near me on the grass lies Glanvil's book –
　　Come, let me read the oft-read tale again,
　　　　The story of that Oxford scholar poor
Of pregnant parts and quick inventive brain,
　　Who, tir'd of knocking at Preferment's door,
　　　　One summer morn forsook
His friends, and went to learn the Gipsy lore,
　　And roam'd the world with that wild brotherhood,
　　And came, as most men deem'd, to little good,
　　　　But came to Oxford and his friends no more.

But once, years after, in the country lanes,
　　Two scholars whom at college erst he knew
　　　　Met him, and of his way of life enquir'd.
Whereat he answer'd, that the Gipsy crew,
　　His mates, had arts to rule as they desir'd
　　　　The workings of men's brains;
And they can bind them to what thoughts they will:
　　'And I,' he said, 'the secret of their art,
　　When fully learn'd, will to the world impart:
　　　　But it needs heaven-sent moments for this skill.'

This said, he left them, and return'd no more,
　　But rumours hung about the country side
　　　　That the lost Scholar long was seen to stray,
Seen by rare glimpses, pensive and tongue-tied,
　　In hat of antique shape, and cloak of grey,
　　　　The same the Gipsies wore.
Shepherds had met him on the Hurst in spring:
　　At some lone alehouse in the Berkshire moors,
　　On the warm ingle beach, the smock-frock'd boors
　　　　Had found him seated at their entering.

But, mid their drink and clatter, he would fly:
    And I myself seem half to know thy looks,
        And put the shepherds, Wanderer, on thy trace;
    And boys who in lone wheatfields scare the rooks
        I ask if thou hast pass'd their quiet place;
            Or in my boat I lie
    Moor'd to the cool bank in the summer heats,
        Mid wide grass meadows which the sunshine fills,
        And watch the warm green-muffled Cumner hills,
            And wonder if thou haunt'st their shy retreats.

For most, I know, thou lov'st retired ground.
    Thee, at the ferry, Oxford riders blithe,
        Returning home on summer nights, have met
    Crossing the stripling Thames at Bab-lock-hithe,
        Trailing in the cool stream thy fingers wet,
            As the slow punt swings round:
    And leaning backwards in a pensive dream,
        And fostering in thy lap a heap of flowers
        Pluck'd in shy fields and distant Wychwood bowers,
            And thine eyes resting on the moonlit stream.

And then they land, and thou art seen no more.
    Maidens who from the distant hamlets come
        To dance around the Fyfield elm in May,
    Oft through the darkening fields have seen thee roam,
        Or cross a stile into the public way.
            Oft thou hast given them store
    Of flowers – the frail-leaf'd, white anemone –
        Dark bluebells drench'd with dews of summer eves –
        And purple orchises with spotted leaves –
            But none has words she can report of thee.

And, above Godstow Bridge, when hay-time's here
    In June, and many a scythe in sunshine flames,
        Men who through those wide fields of breezy grass
    Where black-wing'd swallows haunt the glittering Thames,
        To bathe in the abandon'd lasher pass,
            Have often pass'd thee near
    Sitting upon the river bank o'ergrown:
        Mark'd thy outlandish garb, thy figure spare,
        Thy dark vague eyes, and soft abstracted air;
            But, when they came from bathing, thou wert gone.

At some lone homestead in the Cumner hills,
    Where at her open door the housewife darns,
        Thou hast been seen, or hanging on a gate
    To watch the threshers in the mossy barns.
        Children, who early range these slopes and late
            For creases from the rills,
    Have known thee watching, all an April day,
        The springing pastures and the feeding kine;
        And mark'd thee, when the stars come out and shine,
            Through the long dewy grass move slow away.

In Autumn, on the skirts of Bagley wood,
    Where most the Gipsies by the turf-edg'd way
        Pitch their smok'd tents, and every bush you see
    With scarlet patches tagg'd and shreds of grey,
        Above the forest ground call'd Thessaly –
            The blackbird picking food
    Sees thee, nor stops his meal, nor fears at all;
        So often has he known thee past him stray
        Rapt, twirling in thy hand a wither'd spray,
            And waiting for the spark from Heaven to fall.

And once, in winter, on the causeway chill
    Where home through flooded fields foot-travellers go,
        Have I not pass'd thee on the wooden bridge
    Wrapt in thy cloak and battling with the snow,
        Thy face towards Hinksey and its wintry ridge?
            And thou hast climb'd the hill
    And gain'd the white brow of the Cumner range,
        Turn'd once to watch, while thick the snowflakes fall,
        The line of festal light in Christ-Church hall –
            Then sought thy straw in some sequester'd grange.

But what – I dream! Two hundred years are flown
    Since first thy story ran through Oxford halls,
        And the grave Glanvil did the tale inscribe
    That thou wert wander'd from the studious walls
        To learn strange arts, and join a Gipsy tribe:
            And thou from earth art gone
    Long since, and in some quiet churchyard laid;
        Some country nook, where o'er thy unknown grave
        Tall grasses and white flowering nettles wave –
            Under a dark red-fruited yew-tree's shade.

– No, no, thou hast not felt the lapse of hours.
   For what wears out the life of mortal men?
      'Tis that from change to change their being rolls:
   'Tis that repeated shocks, again, again,
      Exhaust the energy of strongest souls,
        And numb the elastic powers.
   Till having us'd our nerves with bliss and teen,
      And tir'd upon a thousand schemes our wit,
      To the just-pausing Genius we remit
        Our worn-out life, and are – what we have been.

Thou hast not liv'd, why should'st thou perish, so?
   Thou hadst *one* aim, *one* business, *one* desire:
      Else wert thou long since number'd with the dead –
   Else hadst thou spent, like other men, thy fire.
      The generations of thy peers are fled,
        And we ourselves shall go;
   But thou possessest an immortal lot,
      And we imagine thee exempt from age
      And living as thou liv'st on Glanvil's page,
        Because thou hadst – what we, alas, have not!

For early didst thou leave the world, with powers
   Fresh, undiverted to the world without,
      Firm to their mark, not spent on other things;
   Free from the sick fatigue, the languid doubt,
      Which much to have tried, in much been baffled, brings.
        O Life unlike to ours!
   Who fluctuate idly without term or scope,
      Of whom each strives, nor knows for what he strives,
      And each half lives a hundred different lives;
        Who wait like thee, but not, like thee, in hope.

Thou waitest for the spark from Heaven: and we,
   Light half-believers of our casual creeds,
      Who never deeply felt, nor clearly will'd,
   Whose insight never has borne fruit in deeds,
      Whose vague resolves never have been fulfill'd;
        For whom each year we see
   Breeds new beginnings, disappointments new;
      Who hesitate and falter life away,
      And lose to-morrow the ground won to-day –
        Ah, do not we, Wanderer, await it too?

Yes, we await it, but it still delays,
And then we suffer; and amongst us One,
Who most has suffer'd, takes dejectedly
His seat upon the intellectual throne;
And all his store of sad experience he
Lays bare of wretched days;
Tells us his misery's birth and growth and signs,
And how the dying spark of hope was fed,
And how the breast was sooth'd, and how the head,
And all his hourly varied anodynes.

This for our wisest: and we others pine,
And wish the long unhappy dream would end,
And waive all claim to bliss, and try to bear
With close-lipp'd Patience for our only friend,
Sad Patience, too near neighbour to Despair:
But none has hope like thine.
Thou through the fields and through the woods dost stray,
Roaming the country side, a truant boy,
Nursing thy project in unclouded joy,
And every doubt long blown by time away.

O born in days when wits were fresh and clear,
And life ran gaily as the sparkling Thames;
Before this strange disease of modern life,
With its sick hurry, its divided aims,
Its heads o'ertax'd, its palsied hearts, was rife –
Fly hence, our contact fear!
Still fly, plunge deeper in the bowering wood!
Averse, as Dido did with gesture stern
From her false friend's approach in Hades turn,
Wave us away, and keep thy solitude.

Still nursing the unconquerable hope,
Still clutching the inviolable shade,
With a free onward impulse brushing through,
By night, the silver'd branches of the glade –
Far on the forest skirts, where none pursue
On some mild pastoral slope
Emerge, and resting on the moonlit pales,
Freshen thy flowers, as in former years,
With dew, or listen with enchanted ears,
From the dark dingles, to the nightingales.

But fly our paths, our feverish contact fly!
    For strong the infection of our mental strife,
        Which, though it gives no bliss, yet spoils for rest;
    And we should win thee from thy own fair life,
        Like us distracted, and like us unblest.
            Soon, soon thy cheer would die,
    Thy hopes grow timorous, and unfix'd thy powers,
        And thy clear aims be cross and shifting made:
        And then thy glad perennial youth would fade,
            Fade, and grow old at last, and die like ours.

Then fly our greetings, fly our speech and smiles!
    – As some grave Tyrian trader, from the sea,
        Descried at sunrise an emerging prow
    Lifting the cool-hair'd creepers stealthily,
        The fringes of a southward-facing brow
            Among the Aegean isles:
    And saw the merry Grecian coaster come,
        Freighted with amber grapes, and Chian wine,
        Green bursting figs, and tunnies steep'd in brine;
            And knew the intruders on his ancient home,

The young light-hearted Masters of the waves;
    And snatch'd his rudder, and shook out more sail,
        And day and night held on indignantly
    O'er the blue Midland waters with the gale,
        Betwixt the Syrtes and soft Sicily,
            To where the Atlantic raves
    Outside the Western Straits, and unbent sails
        There, where down cloudy cliffs, through sheets of foam,
        Shy traffickers, the dark Iberians come:
            And on the beech undid his corded bales.

Dover Beach

The sea is calm to-night,
The tide is full, the moon lies fair
Upon the Straits; – on the French coast, the light
Gleams, and is gone; the cliffs of England stand,

Glimmering and vast, out in the tranquil bay.
Come to the window, sweet is the night air!
Only, from the long line of spray
Where the ebb meets the moon-blanch'd sand,
Listen! you hear the grating roar
Of pebbles which the waves suck back, and fling,
At their return, up the high strand,
Begin, and cease, and then again begin,
With tremulous cadence slow, and bring
The eternal note of sadness in.

Sophocles long ago
Heard it on the Aegaean, and it brought
Into his mind the turbid ebb and flow
Of human misery; we
Find also in the sound a thought,
Hearing it by this distant northern sea.

The sea of faith
Was once, too, at the full, and round earth's shore
Lay like the folds of a bright girdle furl'd;
But now I only hear
Its melancholy, long, withdrawing roar,
Retreating to the breath
Of the night-wind down the vast edges drear
And naked shingles of the world.

Ah, love, let us be true
To one another! for the world, which seems
To lie before us like a land of dreams,
So various, so beautiful, so new,
Hath really neither joy, nor love, nor light,
Nor certitude, nor peace, nor help for pain;
And we are here as on a darkling plain
Swept with confused alarms of struggle and flight,
Where ignorant armies clash by night.

DANTE GABRIEL ROSSETTI

During Music

O cool unto the sense of pain
    That last night's sleep could not destroy;
    O warm unto the sense of joy,
That dreams its life within the brain.

What though I lean o'er thee to scan
    The written music cramped and stiff; –
    'Tis dark to me, as hieroglyph
On those weird bulks Egyptian.

But as from those, dumb now and strange,
    A glory wanders on the earth,
    Even so thy tones can call a birth
From these, to shake my soul with change.

O swift, as in melodious haste
    Float o'er the keys thy fingers small;
    O soft, as is the rise and fall
Which stirs that shade within thy breast.

The Honeysuckle

I plucked a honeysuckle where
    The hedge on high is quick with thorn,
    And climbing for the prize, was torn,
And fouled my feet in quag-water;
    And by the thorns and by the wind
    The blossom that I took was thinn'd,
And yet I found it sweet and fair.

Thence to a richer growth I came,
    Where, nursed in mellow intercourse,
    The honeysuckles sprang by scores,

Not harried like my single stem,
　　All virgin lamps of scent and dew.
　　So from my hand that first I threw,
Yet plucked not any more of them.

Sudden Light

　　I have been here before,
　　　　But when or how I cannot tell:
　　I know the grass beyond the door,
　　　　The sweet, keen smell,
The sighing sound, the lights around the shore.

　　You have been mine before, –
　　　　How long ago I may not know:
　　But just when at that swallow's soar
　　　　Your neck turned so,
Some veil did fall, – I knew it all of yore.

　　Has this been thus before?
　　　　And shall not thus time's eddying flight
　　Still with our lives our love restore
　　　　In death's despite,
And day and night yield one delight once more?

The Woodspurge

The wind flapped loose, the wind was still,
Shaken out dead from tree and hill:
I had walked on at the wind's will, –
I sat now, for the wind was still.

Between my knees my forehead was, –
My lips, drawn in, said not Alas!
My hair was over in the grass,
My naked ears heard the day pass.

150

My eyes, wide open, had the run
Of some ten weeds to fix upon;
Among those few, out of the sun,
The woodspurge flowered, three cups in one.

From perfect grief there need not be
Wisdom or even memory:
One thing then learnt remains to me, –
The woodspurge has a cup of three.

A Little While

A little while a little love
   The hour yet bears for thee and me
   Who have not drawn the veil to see
If still our heaven be lit above.
Thou merely, at the day's last sigh,
   Hast felt thy soul prolong the tone;
And I have heard the night-wind cry
     And deemed its speech mine own.

A little while a little love
   The scattering autumn hoards for us
   Whose bower is not yet ruinous
Nor quite unleaved our songless grove.
Only across the shaken boughs
   We hear the flood-tides seek the sea,
And deep in both our hearts they rouse
     One wail for thee and me.

A little while a little love
   May yet be ours who have not said
   The word it makes our eyes afraid
To know that each is thinking of.
Not yet the end: be our lips dumb
   In smiles a little season yet:
I'll tell thee, when the end is come,
     How we may best forget.

Sunset Wings

Tonight this sunset spreads two golden wings
   Cleaving the western sky;
Winged too with wind it is, and winnowings
Of birds; as if the day's last hour in rings
   Of strenuous flight must die.

Sun-steeped in fire, the homeward pinions sway
   Above the dovecote-tops;
And clouds of starlings, ere they rest with day,
Sink, clamorous like mill-waters, at wild play,
   By turns in every copse:

Each tree heart-deep the wrangling rout receives, –
   Save for the whirr within,
You could not tell the starlings from the leaves;
Then one great puff of wings, and the swarm heaves
   Away with all its din.

Even thus Hope's hours, in ever-eddying flight,
   To many a refuge tend;
With the first light she laughed, and the last light
Glows round her still; who natheless in the night
   At length must make an end.

And now the mustering rooks innumerable
   Together sail and soar,
While for the day's death, like a tolling knell,
Unto the heart they seem to cry, Farewell,
   No more, farewell, no more!

Is Hope not plumed, as 'twere a fiery dart?
   And oh! thou dying day,
Even as thou goest must she too depart,
And Sorrow fold such pinions on the heart
   As will not fly away?

Three Shadows

I looked and saw your eyes
  In the shadow of your hair
As a traveller sees the stream
  In the shadow of the wood;
And I said, 'My faint heart sighs
  Ah me! to linger there,
To drink deep and to dream
  In that sweet solitude.'

I looked and saw your heart
  In the shadow of your eyes,
As a seeker sees the gold
  In the shadow of the stream;
And I said, 'Ah me! what art
  Should win the immortal prize,
Whose want must make life cold
  And Heaven a hollow dream?'

I looked and saw your love
  In the shadow of your heart,
As a diver sees the pearl
  In the shadow of the sea;
And I murmured, not above
  My breath, but all apart, –
'Ah! you can love, true girl,
  And is your love for me?'

CHRISTINA ROSSETTI

A Birthday

My heart is like a singing bird
    Whose nest is in a watered shoot:
My heart is like an apple-tree
    Whose boughs are bent with thickset fruit;
My heart is like a rainbow shell
    That paddles in a halcyon sea;
My heart is gladder than all these
    Because my love is come to me.

Raise me a dais of silk and down;
    Hang it with vair and purple dyes;
Carve it in doves and pomegranates,
    And peacocks with a hundred eyes;
Work it in gold and silver grapes,
    In leaves and silver fleur-de-lys;
Because the birthday of my life
    Is come, my love is come to me.

EMILY DICKINSON

Exultation is the going
Of an inland soul to sea,
Past the houses – past the headlands –
Into deep Eternity –

Bred as we, among the mountains,
Can the sailor understand
The divine intoxication
Of the first league out from land?

I never hear the word 'escape'
Without a quicker blood,
A sudden expectation,
A flying attitude!

I never hear of prisons broad
By soldiers battered down,
But I tug childish at my bars
Only to fail again!

There's a certain Slant of light,
Winter Afternoons –
That oppresses, like the Heft
Of Cathedral Tunes –

Heavenly Hurt, it gives us –
We can find no scar,
But internal difference,
Where the Meanings, are –

None may teach it – Any –
'Tis the Seal Despair –
An imperial affliction
Sent us of the Air –

When it comes, the Landscape listens –
Shadows – hold their breath –
When it goes, 'tis like the Distance
On the look of Death –

It might be lonelier
Without the Loneliness –
I'm so accustomed to my Fate –
Perhaps the Other – Peace –

Would interrupt the Dark –
And crowd the little Room –
Too scant – by Cubits – to contain
The Sacrament – of Him –

I am not used to Hope –
It might intrude upon –
Its sweet parade – blaspheme the place –
Ordained to Suffering –

It might be easier
To fail – with Land in Sight –
Than gain – My Blue Peninsula –
To perish – of Delight –

We grow accustomed to the Dark –
When Light is put away –
As when the Neighbor holds the Lamp
To witness her Goodbye –

A Moment – We uncertain step
For newness of the night –
Then – fit our Vision to the Dark –
And meet the Road – erect –

And so of larger – Darknesses –
Those Evenings of the Brain –
When not a Moon disclose a sign –
Or Star – come out – within –

The Bravest – grope a little –
And sometimes hit a Tree
Directly in the Forehead –
But as they learn to see –

Either the Darkness alters –
Or something in the sight
Adjusts itself to Midnight –
And Life steps almost straight.

This is my letter to the World
That never wrote to Me –
The simple News that Nature told –
With tender Majesty

Her Message is committed
To Hands I cannot see –
For love of Her – Sweet – countrymen –
Judge tenderly – of Me

It was not Death, for I stood up,
And all the Dead, lie down –
It was not Night, for all the Bells
Put out their Tongues, for Noon.

It was not Frost, for on my Flesh
I felt Siroccos – crawl –
Nor Fire – for just my Marble feet
Could keep a Chancel, cool –

And yet, it tasted, like them all,
The Figures I have seen
Set orderly, for Burial,
Reminded me, of mine –

As if my life were shaven,
And fitted to a frame,
And could not breathe without a key,
And 'twas like Midnight, some –

When everything that ticked – has stopped –
And Space stares all around –
Or Grisly frosts – first Autumn morns,
Repeal the Beating Ground –

But, most, like Chaos – Stopless – cool –
Without a Chance, or Spar –
Or even a Report of Land –
To justify – Despair.

GERARD MANLEY HOPKINS

from *The Wreck of the Deutschland*

To the
happy memory of five Franciscan Nuns
exiles by the Falk Laws
drowned between midnight and morning of
Dec. 7th, 1875

PART THE FIRST

1

Thou mastering me
God! giver of breath and bread;
World's strand, sway of the sea;
Lord of living and dead;
Thou hast bound bones and veins in me, fastened me flesh,
And after it almost unmade, what with dread,
Thy doing: and dost thou touch me afresh?
Over again I feel thy finger and find thee.

2

I did say yes
O at lightning and lashed rod;
Thou heardst me truer than tongue confess
Thy terror, O Christ, O God;
Thou knowest the walls, altar and hour and night:
The swoon of a heart that the sweep and the hurl of thee trod
Hard down with a horror of height:
And the midriff astrain with leaning of, laced with fire of stress.

3

The frown of his face
Before me, the hurtle of hell
Behind, where, where was a, where was a place?
I whirled out wings that spell

159

And fled with a fling of the heart to the heart of the Host.
My heart, but you were dovewinged, I can tell,
    Carrier-witted, I am bold to boast,
To flash from the flame to the flame then, tower from the grace to the
    grace.

4

I am soft sift
In an hourglass – at the wall
Fast, but mined with a motion, a drift,
    And it crowds and it combs to the fall;
I steady as a water in a well, to a poise, to a pane,
But roped with, always, all the way down from the tall
    Fells or flanks of the voel, a vein
Of the gospel proffer, a pressure, a principle, Christ's gift.

5

I kiss my hand
To the stars, lovely-asunder
Starlight, wafting him out of it; and
    Glow, glory in thunder;
Kiss my hand to the dappled-with-damson west:
Since, tho' he is under the world's splendour and wonder,
    His mystery must be instressed, stressed;
For I greet him the days I meet him, and bless when I understand.

6

Not out of his bliss
Springs the stress felt
Nor first from heaven (and few know this)
    Swings the stroke dealt –
Stroke and a stress that stars and storms deliver,
That guilt is hushed by, hearts are flushed by and melt –
    But it rides time like riding a river
(And here the faithful waver, the faithless fable and miss).

7

It dates from day
Of his going in Galilee;
Warm-laid grave of a womb-life grey;
Manger, maiden's knee;
The dense and the driven Passion, and frightful sweat;
Thence the discharge of it, there its swelling to be,
Though felt before, though in high flood yet –
What none would have known of it, only the heart, being hard at bay,

8

Is out with it! Oh,
We lash with the best or worst
Word last! How a lush-kept plush-capped sloe
Will, mouthed to flesh-burst,
Gush! – flush the man, the being with it, sour or sweet,
Brim, in a flash, full! – Hither then, last or first,
To hero of Calvary, Christ's feet –
Never ask if meaning it, wanting it, warned of it – men go.

9

Be adored among men,
God, three-numberèd form;
Wring thy rebel, dogged in den,
Man's malice, with wrecking and storm.
Beyond saying sweet, past telling of tongue,
Thou art lightning and love, I found it, a winter and warm;
Father and fondler of heart thou hast wrung:
Hast thy dark descending and most art merciful then.

10

With an anvil-ding
And with fire in him forge thy will
Or rather, rather then, stealing as Spring
Through him, melt him but master him still:
Whether at once, as once at a crash Paul,
Or as Austin, a lingering-out sweet skill,
Make mercy in all of us, out of us all
Mastery, but be adored, but be adored King.

161

32

I admire thee, master of the tides,
Of the Yore-flood, of the year's fall;
The recurb and the recovery of the gulf's sides,
The girth of it and the wharf of it and the wall;
Stanching, quenching ocean of a motionable mind;
Ground of being, and granite of it: past all
Grasp God, throned behind
Death with a sovereignty that heeds but hides, bodes but abides;

33

With a mercy that outrides
The all of water, an ark
For the listener; for the lingerer with a love glides
Lower than death and the dark;
A vein for the visiting of the past-prayer, pent in prison,
The-last-breath penitent spirits – the uttermost mark
Our passion-plungèd giant risen,
The Christ of the Father compassionate, fetched in the storm of his
strides.

34

Now burn, new born to the world,
Doubled-naturèd name,
The heaven-flung, heart-fleshed, maiden-furled
Miracle-in-Mary-of-flame,
Mid-numbered He in three of the thunder-throne!
Not a dooms-day dazzle in his coming nor dark as he came;
Kind, but royally reclaiming his own;
A released shower, let flash to the shire, not a lightning of fire hard-hurled.

35

Dame, at our door
Drowned, and among our shoals,
Remember us in the roads, the heaven-haven of the Reward:

Our King back, oh, upon English souls!
Let him easter in us, be a dayspring to the dimness of us, be a
crimson-cresseted east,
More brightening her, rare-dear Britain, as his reign rolls,
Pride, rose, prince, hero of us, high-priest,
Our hearts' charity's hearth's fire, our thoughts' chivalry's throng's Lord.

God's Grandeur

The world is charged with the grandeur of God.
It will flame out, like shining from shook foil;
It gathers to a greatness, like the ooze of oil
Crushed. Why do men then now not reck his rod?
Generations have trod, have trod, have trod;
And all is seared with trade, bleared, smeared with toil;
And wears man's smudge and shares man's smell: the soil
Is bare now, nor can foot feel, being shod.

And for all this, nature is never spent;
There lives the dearest freshness deep down things;
And though the last lights off the black West went
Oh, morning, at the brown brink eastward, springs –
Because the Holy Ghost over the bent
World broods with warm breast and with ah! bright wings.

Spring

Nothing is so beautiful as spring –
When weeds, in wheels, shoot long and lovely and lush;
Thrush's eggs look little low heavens, and thrush
Through the echoing timber does so rinse and wring
The ear, it strikes like lightnings to hear him sing;
The glassy peartree leaves and blooms, they brush
The descending blue; that blue is all in a rush
With richness; the racing lambs too have fair their fling.

What is all this juice and all this joy?
   A strain of the earth's sweet being in the beginning
In Eden garden, – Have, get, before it cloy,
   Before it cloud, Christ, lord, and sour with sinning,
Innocent mind and Mayday in girl and boy,
   Most, O maid's child, thy choice and worthy the winning.

The Lantern out of Doors

Sometimes a lantern moves along the night,
   That interests our eyes. And who goes there?
   I think; where from and bound, I wonder, where,
With, all down darkness wide, his wading light?

Men go by me whom either beauty bright
   In mould or mind or what not else makes rare:
   They rain against our much-thick and marsh air
Rich beams, till death or distance buys them quite.

Death or distance soon consumes them: wind
   What most I may eye after, be in at the end
I cannot, and out of sight is out of mind.

Christ minds; Christ's interest, what to avow or amend
   There, éyes them, heart wánts, care haúnts, foot fóllows kínd,
Their ránsom, théir rescue, ánd first, fást, last friénd.

The Windhover:

To Christ our Lord

I caught this morning morning's minion, king-
   dom of daylight's dauphin, dapple-dawn-drawn Falcon, in his riding
   Of the rolling level underneath him steady air, and striding
High there, how he rung upon the rein of a wimpling wing

In his ecstasy! then off, off forth on swing,
As a skate's heel sweeps smooth on a bow-bend: the hurl and gliding
Rebuffed the big wind. My heart in hiding
Stirred for a bird, – the achieve of, the mastery of the thing!

Brute beauty and valour and act, oh, air, pride, plume, here
Buckle! and the fire that breaks from thee then, a billion
Times told lovelier, more dangerous, O my chevalier!

No wonder of it: shéer plód makes plough down sillion
Shine, and blue-bleak embers, ah my dear,
Fall, gall themselves, and gash gold-vermilion.

Duns Scotus's Oxford

Towery city and branchy between towers;
Cuckoo-echoing, bell-swarmèd, lark-charmèd, rook-racked, river-
rounded;
The dapple-eared lily below thee; that country and town did
Once encounter in, here coped and poisèd powers;

Thou hast a base and brickish skirt there, sours
That neighbour-nature thy grey beauty is grounded
Best in; graceless growth, thou hast confounded
Rural rural keeping – folk, flocks, and flowers.

Yet ah! this air I gather and I release
He lived on; these weeds and waters, these walls are what
He haunted who of all men most sways my spirits to peace;

Of realty the rarest-veinèd unraveller; a not
Rivalled insight, be rival Italy or Greece;
Who fired France for Mary without spot.

Brothers

How lovely the elder brother's
Life all laced in the other's,
Lóve-laced! – what once I well
Witnessed; so fortune fell.
When Shrovetide, two years gone,
Our boys' plays bróught on
Part was picked for John,
Young Jóhn: then fear, then joy
Ran revel in the elder boy.
Their night was come now; all
Our company thronged the hall;
Henry, by the wall,
Beckoned me beside him:
I came where called, and eyed him
By meanwhiles; making mý play
Turn most on tender byplay.
For, wrung all on love's rack,
My lad, and lost in Jack,
Smiled, blushed, and bit his lip;
Or drove, with a diver's dip,
Clutched hands down through clasped knees –
Truth's tokens tricks like these,
Old telltales, with what stress
He hung on the imp's success.
Now the other was bráss-bóld:
Hé had no work to hold
His heart up at the strain;
Nay, roguish ran the vein.
Two tedious acts were past;
Jack's call and cue at last;
When Henry, heart-forsook,
Dropped eyes and dared not look.
Eh, how áll rúng!
Young dog, he did give tongue!
But Harry – in his hands he has flung
His tear-tricked cheeks of flame
For fond love and for shame.
　　Ah Nature, framed in fault,
There 's comfort then, there 's salt;
Nature, bad, base, and blind,

166

Dearly thou canst be kind;
There dearly thén, deárly,
I'll cry thou canst be kind.

'As kingfishers catch fire'

As kingfishers catch fire, dragonflies dráw fláme;
As tumbled over rim in roundy wells
Stones ring; like each tucked string tells, each hung bell's
Bow swung finds tongue to fling out broad its name;
Each mortal thing does one thing and the same:
Deals out that being indoors each one dwells;
Selves – goes itself; *myself* it speaks and spells,
Crying *Whát I do is me: for that I came.*

Í say móre: the just man justices;
Kéeps gráce: thát keeps all his goings graces;
Acts in God's eye what in God's eye he is –
Chríst – for Christ plays in ten thousand places,
Lovely in lumbs, and lovely in eyes not his
To the Father through the features of men's faces.

The Blessed Virgin compared to the Air we Breathe

Wild air, world-mothering air,
Nestling me everywhere,
That each eyelash or hair
Girdles; goes home betwixt
The fleeciest, frailest-flixed
Snowflake; that's fairly mixed
With, riddles, and is rife
In every least thing's life;
This needful, never spent,
And nursing element;
My more than meat and drink,

My meal at every wink;
This air, which, by life's law,
My lung must draw and draw
Now but to breathe its praise,
Minds me in many ways
Of her who not only
Gave God's infinity
Dwindled to infancy
Welcome in womb and breast,
Birth, milk, and all the rest
But mothers each new grace
That does now reach our race –
Mary Immaculate,
Merely a woman, yet
Whose presence, power is
Great as no goddess's
Was deemèd, dreamèd; who
This one work has to do –
Let all God's glory through,
God's glory which would go
Through her and from her flow
Off, and no way but so.

    I say that we are wound
With mercy round and round
As if with air: the same
Is Mary, more by name.
She, wild web, wondrous robe,
Mantles the guilty globe,
Since God has let dispense
Her prayers his providence:
Nay, more than almoner,
The sweet alms' self is her
And men are meant to share
Her life as life does air.
    If I have understood,
She holds high motherhood
Towards all our ghostly good
And plays in grace her part
About man's beating heart,
Laying, like air's fine flood,
The deathdance in his blood;

Yet no part but what will
Be Christ our Saviour still.
Of her flesh he took flesh:
He does take fresh and fresh,
Though much the mystery how,
Not flesh but spirit now
And makes, O marvellous!
New Nazareths in us,
Where she shall yet conceive
Him, morning, noon, and eve;
New Bethlems, and he born
There, evening, noon, and morn –
Bethlem or Nazareth,
Men here may draw like breath
More Christ and baffle death;
Who, born so, comes to be
New self and nobler me
In each one and each one
More makes, when all is done,
Both God's and Mary's Son.

    Again, look overhead
How air is azurèd;
O how! nay do but stand
Where you can lift your hand
Skywards: rich, rich it laps
Round the four fingertips.
Yet such a sapphire-shot,
Charged, steepèd sky will not
Stain light. Yea, mark you this:
It does no prejudice.
The glass-blue days are those
When every colour glows,
Each shape and shadow shows.
Blue be it: this blue heaven
The seven or seven times seven
Hued sunbeam will transmit
Perfect, not alter it.
Or if there does some soft,
On things aloof, aloft,
Bloom breathe, that one breath more
Earth is the fairer for.
Whereas did air not make

169

This bath of blue and slake
His fire, the sun would shake,
A blear and blinding ball
With blackness bound, and all
The thick stars round him roll
Flashing like flecks of coal,
Quartz-fret, or sparks of salt,
In grimy vasty vault.

    So God was god of old:
A mother came to mould
Those limbs like ours which are
What must make our daystar
Much dearer to mankind;
Whose glory bare would blind
Or less would win man's mind.
Through her we may see him
Made sweeter, not made dim,
And her hand leaves his light
Sifted to suit our sight.

    Be thou then, O thou dear
Mother, my atmosphere;
My happier world, wherein
To wend and meet no sin;
Above me, round me lie
Fronting my froward eye
With sweet and scarless sky;
Stir in my ears, speak there
Of God's love, O live air,
Of patience, penance, prayer:
World-mothering air, air wild,
Wound with thee, in thee isled,
Fold home, fast fold thy child.

'I wake and feel the fell of dark'

I wake and feel the fell of dark, not day.
What hours, O what black hoürs we have spent
This night! what sights you, heart, saw; ways you went!
And more must, in yet longer light's delay.

  With witness I speak this. But where I say
Hours I mean years, mean life. And my lament
Is cries countless, cries like dead letters sent
To dearest him that lives alas! away.

  I am gall, I am heartburn. God's most deep decree
Bitter would have me taste: my taste was me;
Bones built in me, flesh filled, blood brimmed the curse.
  Selfyeast of spirit a dull dough sours. I see
The lost are like this, and their scourge to be
As I am mine, their sweating selves; but worse.

'My own heart let me more have pity on'

My own heart let me more have pity on; let
Me live to my sad self hereafter kind,
Charitable; not live this tormented mind
With this tormented mind tormenting yet.

  I cast for comfort I can no more get
By groping round my comfortless, than blind
Eyes in their dark can day or thirst can find
Thirst 's all-in-all in all a world of wet.

Soul, self; come, poor Jackself, I do advise
You, jaded, let be; call off thoughts awhile
Elsewhere; leave comfort root-room; let joy size
At God knows when to God knows what; whose smile
's not wrung, see you; unforeseen times rather – as skies
Betweenpie mountains – lights a lovely mile.

In honour of
St Alphonsus Rodriguez
Laybrother of the Society of Jesus

Honour is flashed off exploit, so we say;
And those strokes once that gashed flesh or galled shield
Should tongue that time now, trumpet now that field,
And, on the fighter, forge his glorious day.
On Christ they do and on the martyr may;
But be the war within, the brand we wield
Unseen, the heroic breast not outward-steeled,
Earth hears no hurtle then from fiercest fray.

   Yet God (that hews mountain and continent,
Earth, all, out; who, with trickling increment,
Veins violets and tall trees makes more and more)
Could crowd career with conquest while there went
Those years and years by of world without event
That in Majorca Alfonso watched the door.

G.K. CHESTERTON

Lepanto

White founts falling in the courts of the sun,
And the Soldan of Byzantium is smiling as they run;
There is laughter like the fountains in that face of all men feared,
It stirs the forest darkness, the darkness of his beard,
It curls the blood-red crescent, the crescent of his lips,
For the inmost sea of all the earth is shaken with his ships.
They have dared the white republics up the capes of Italy,
They have dashed the Adriatic round the Lion of the Sea,
And the Pope has cast his arms abroad for agony and loss,
And called the kings of Christendom for swords about the Cross,
The cold queen of England is looking in the glass;
The shadow of the Valois is yawning at the Mass;

From evening isles fantastical rings faint the Spanish gun,
And the Lord upon the Golden Horn is laughing in the sun.

Dim drums throbbing, in the hills half heard,
Where only on a nameless throne a crownless prince has stirred,
Where, risen from a doubtful seat and half-attainted stall,
The last knight of Europe takes weapons from the wall,
The last and lingering troubadour to whom the bird had sung,
That once went singing southward when all the world was young,
In that enormous silence, tiny and unafraid,
Comes up along a winding road the noise of the Crusade.
Strong gongs groaning as the guns boom far,
Don John of Austria is going to the war,
Stiff flags straining in the night-blasts cold
In the gloom black-purple, in the glint old-gold,
Torchlight crimson on the copper kettle-drums,
Then the tuckets, then the trumpets, then the cannon, and he comes.
Don John laughing in the brave beard curled,
Spurning of his stirrups like the thrones of all the world,
Holding his head up for a flag of all the free.
Love-light of Spain – hurrah!
Death-light of Africa!
Don John of Austria
Is riding to the sea.

Mahound is in his paradise above the evening star,
(*Don John of Austria is going to the war.*)
He moves a mighty turban on the timeless houri's knees,
His turban that is woven of the sunset and the seas.
He shakes the peacock gardens as he rises from his ease,
And he strides among the tree-tops and is taller than the trees,
And his voice through all the garden is a thunder sent to bring
Black Azrael and Ariel and Ammon on the wing.
Giants and the Genii,
Multiplex of wing and eye,
Whose strong obedience broke the sky
When Solomon was king.

They rush in red and purple from the red clouds of the morn,
From temples where the yellow gods shut up their eyes in scorn;
They rise in green robes roaring from the green hells of the sea
Where fallen skies and evil hues and eyeless creatures be;

173

On them the sea-valves cluster and the grey sea-forests curl,
Splashed with a splendid sickness, the sickness of the pearl;
They swell in sapphire smoke out of the blue cracks of the ground, –
They gather and they wonder and give worship to Mahound.
And he saith, 'Break up the mountains where the hermit-folk can hide,
And sift the red and silver sands lest bone of saint abide,
And chase the Giaours flying night and day, not giving rest,
For that which was our trouble comes again out of the west.
We have set the seal of Solomon on all things under sun,
Of knowledge and of sorrow and endurance of things done,
But a noise is in the mountains, in the mountains, and I know
The voice that shook our palaces – four hundred years ago:
It is he that saith not 'Kismet'; it is he that knows not Fate;
It is Richard, it is Raymond, it is Godfrey in the gate!
It is he whose loss is laughter when he counts the wager worth,
Put down your feet upon him, that our peace be on the earth.'
For he heard drums groaning and he heard guns jar,
(*Don John of Austria is going to the war.*)
Sudden and still – hurrah!
Bolt from Iberia!
Don John of Austria
Is gone by Alcalar.

St Michael's on his mountain in the sea-roads of the north
(*Don John of Austria is girt and going forth.*)
Where the grey seas glitter and the sharp tides shift
And the sea folk labour and the red sails lift.
He shakes his lance of iron and he claps his wings of stone;
The noise is gone through Normandy; the noise is gone alone;
The North is full of tangled things and texts and aching eyes
And dead is all the innocence of anger and surprise,
And Christian killeth Christian in a narrow dusty room,
And Christian dreadeth Christ that hath a newer face of doom,
And Christian hateth Mary that God kissed in Galilee,
But Don John of Austria is riding to the sea.
Don John calling through the blast and the eclipse
Crying with the trumpet, with the trumpet of his lips,
Trumpet that sayeth ha!
Domino gloria!
Don John of Austria
Is shouting to the ships.

King Philip's in his closet with the Fleece about his neck
(*Don John of Austria is armed upon the deck.*)
The walls are hung with velvet that is black and soft as sin,
And little dwarfs creep out of it and little dwarfs creep in.
He holds a crystal phial that has colours like the moon,
He touches, and it tingles, and he trembles very soon,
And his face is as a fungus of a leprous white and grey
Like plants in the high houses that are shuttered from the day,
And death is in the phial, and the end of noble work,
But Don John of Austria has fired upon the Turk.
Don John's hunting, and his hounds have bayed –
Booms away past Italy the rumour of his raid
Gun upon gun, ha! ha!
Gun upon gun, hurrah!
Don John of Austria
Has loosed his cannonade.

The Pope was in his chapel before day or battle broke,
(*Don John of Austria is hidden in the smoke.*)
The hidden room in man's house where God sits all the year,
The secret window whence the world looks small and very dear.
He sees as in a mirror on the monstrous twilight sea
The crescent of his cruel ships whose name is mystery;
They fling great shadows foe-wards, making Cross and Castle dark,
They veil the plumèd lions on the galleys of St Mark;
And above the ships are palaces of brown, black-bearded chiefs,
And below the ships are prisons, where with multitudinous griefs,
Christian captives sick and sunless, all a labouring race repines
Like a race in sunken cities, like a nation in the mines.
They are lost like slaves that swat, and in the skies of morning hung
The stair-ways of the tallest gods when tyranny was young.
They are countless, voiceless, hopeless as those fallen or fleeing on
Before the high Kings' horses in the granite of Babylon.
And many a one grows witless in his quiet room in hell
Where a yellow face looks inward through the lattice of his cell,
And he finds his God forgotten, and he seeks no more a sign –
(*But Don John of Austria has burst the battle-line!*)
Don John pounding from the slaughter-painted poop,
Purpling all the ocean like a bloody pirate's sloop,
Scarlet running over on the silvers and the golds,
Breaking of the hatches up and bursting of the holds,
Thronging of the thousands up that labour under sea

White for bliss and blind for sun and stunned for liberty.
Vivat Hispania!
Domino Gloria!
Don John of Austria
Has set his people free!

Cervantes on his galley sets the sword back in the sheath
(*Don John of Austria rides homeward with a wreath.*)
And he sees across a weary land a straggling road in Spain,
Up which a lean and foolish knight forever rides in vain,
And he smiles, but not as Sultans smile, and settles back the blade...
(*But Don John of Austria rides home from the Crusade.*)

The Last Hero

The wind blew out from Bergen from the dawning to the day,
There was a wreck of trees and fall of towers a score of miles away,
And drifted like a livid leaf I go before its tide,
Spewed out of house and stable, beggared of flag and bride.
The heavens are bowed about my head, shouting like seraph wars,
With rains that might put out the sun and clean the sky of stars,
Rains like the fall of ruined seas from secret worlds above,
The roaring of the rains of God none but the lonely love.
Feast in my hall, O foemen, and eat and drink and drain,
You never loved the sun in heaven as I have loved the rain.

The chance of battle changes – so may all battle be;
I stole my lady bride from them, they stole her back from me.
I rent her from her red-roofed hall, I rode and saw arise
More lovely than the living flowers the hatred in her eyes.
She never loved me, never bent, never was less divine;
The sunset never loved me; the wind was never mine.
Was it all nothing that she stood imperial in duresse?
Silence itself made softer with the sweeping of her dress.
O you who drain the cup of life, O you who wear the crown,
You never loved a woman's smile as I have loved her frown.

The wind blew out from Bergen from the dawning to the day,
They ride and run with fifty spears to break and bar my way.

I shall not die alone, alone, but kin to all the powers,
As merry as the ancient sun and fighting like the flowers.
How white their steel, how bright their eyes! I love each laughing knave,
Cry high and bid him welcome to the banquet of the brave.
Yea, I will bless them as they bend and love them where they lie,
When on their skulls the sword I swing falls shattering from the sky.
The hour when death is like a light and blood is like a rose, –
You never loved your friends, my friends, as I shall love my foes.

Know you what earth shall lose tonight, what rich uncounted loans,
What heavy gold of tales untold you bury with my bones?
My loves in deep dim meadows, my ships that rode at ease,
Ruffling the purple plumage of strange and secret seas.
To see this fair earth as it is to me alone was given,
The blow that breaks my brow tonight shall break the dome of heaven.
The skies I saw, the trees I saw after no eyes shall see.
Tonight I die the death of God: the stars shall die with me:
One sound shall sunder all the spears and break the trumpet's breath:
You never laughed in all your life as I shall laugh in death.

EDWARD THOMAS

The Owl

Downhill I came, hungry, and yet not starved;
Cold, yet had heat within me that was proof
Against the North wind; tired, yet so that rest
Had seemed the sweetest thing under a roof.

Then at the inn I had food, fire, and rest,
Knowing how hungry, cold, and tired was I.
All of the night was quite barred out except
An owl's cry, a most melancholy cry

Shaken out long and clear upon the hill,
No merry note, nor cause of merriment,
But one telling me plain what I escaped
And others could not, that night, as in I went.

And salted was my food, and my repose,
Salted and sobered, too, by the bird's voice
Speaking for all who lay under the stars,
Soldiers and poor, unable to rejoice.

Like the Touch of Rain

Like the touch of rain she was
On a man's flesh and hair and eyes
When the joy of walking thus
Has taken him by surprise:

With the love of the storm he burns,
He sings, he laughs, well I know how,
But forgets when he returns
As I shall not forget her 'Go now'.

Those two words shut a door
Between me and the blessed rain
That was never shut before
And will not open again.

And You, Helen

And you, Helen, what should I give you?
So many things I would give you
Had I an infinite great store
Offered me and I stood before
To choose. I would give you youth,
All kinds of loveliness and truth,
A clear eye as good as mine,
Lands, waters, flowers, wine,
As many children as your heart
Might wish for, a far better art
Than mine can be, all you have lost
Upon the travelling waters tossed,

Or given to me. If I could choose
Freely in that great treasure-house
Anything from any shelf,
I would give you back yourself,
And power to discriminate
What you want and want it not too late,
Many fair days free from care
And heart to enjoy both foul and fair,
And myself, too, if I could find
Where it lay hidden and it proved kind.

Rain

Rain, midnight rain, nothing but the wild rain
On this bleak hut, and solitude, and me
Remembering again that I shall die
And neither hear the rain nor give it thanks
For washing me cleaner than I have been
Since I was born into this solitude.
Blessed are the dead that the rain rains upon:
But here I pray that none whom once I loved
Is dying to-night or lying still awake
Solitary, listening to the rain,
Either in pain or thus in sympathy
Helpless among the living and the dead,
Like a cold water among broken reeds,
Myriads of broken reeds all still and stiff,
Like me who have no love which this wild rain
Has not dissolved except the love of death,
If love it be for what is perfect and
Cannot, the tempest tells me, disappoint.

Lights Out

I have come to the borders of sleep,
The unfathomable deep
Forest where all must lose
Their way, however straight,
Or winding, soon or late;
They cannot choose.

Many a road and track
That, since the dawn's first crack,
Up to the forest brink,
Deceived the travellers,
Suddenly now blurs,
And in they sink.

Here love ends,
Despair, ambition ends;
All pleasure and all trouble,
Although most sweet or bitter,
Here ends in sleep that is sweeter
Than tasks more noble.

There is not any book
Or face of dearest look
That I would not turn from now
To go into the unknown
I must enter, and leave, alone,
I know not how.

The tall forest towers;
Its cloudy foliage lowers
Ahead, shelf above shelf;
Its silence I hear and obey
That I may lose my way
And myself.

Words

Out of us all
That make rhymes,
Will you choose
Sometimes –
As the winds use
A crack in a wall
Or a drain,
Their joy or their pain
To whistle through –
Choose me,
You English words?

I know you:
You are light as dreams,
Tough as oak,
Precious as gold,
As poppies and corn,
Or an old cloak:
Sweet as our birds
To the ear,
As the burnet rose
In the heat
Of Midsummer:
Strange as the races
Of dead and unborn:
Strange and sweet
Equally,
And familiar,
To the eye,
As the dearest faces
That a man knows,
And as lost homes are:
But though older far
Than oldest yew, –
As our hills are, old, –
Worn new
Again and again:
Young as our streams
After rain:
And as dear

181

As the earth which you prove
That we love.

Make me content
With some sweetness
From Wales
Whose nightingales
Have no wings, –
From Wiltshire and Kent
And Herefordshire,
And the villages there, –
From the names, and the things
No less.
Let me sometimes dance
With you,
Or climb
Or stand perchance
In ecstasy,
Fixed and free
In a rhyme,
As poets do.

Snow

In the gloom of whiteness,
In the great silence of snow,
A child was sighing
And bitterly saying: 'Oh,
They have killed a white bird up there on her nest,
The down is fluttering from her breast!'
And still it fell through that dusky brightness
On the child crying for the bird of the snow.

No One So Much As You

No one so much as you
Loves this my clay,
Or would lament as you
Its dying day.

You know me through and through
Though I have not told,
And though with what you know
You are not bold.

None ever was so fair
As I thought you:
Not a word can I bear
Spoken against you.

All that I ever did
For you seemed coarse
Compared with what I hid
Nor put in force.

My eyes scarce dare meet you
Lest they should prove
I but respond to you
And do not love.

We look and understand,
We cannot speak
Except in trifles and
Words the most weak.

For I at most accept
Your love, regretting
That is all: I have kept
Only a fretting

That I could not return
All that you gave
And could not ever burn
With the love you have,

Till sometimes it did seem
Better it were
Never to see you more
Than linger here

With only gratitude
Instead of love –
A pine in solitude
Cradling a dove.

Out in the Dark

Out in the dark over the snow
The fallow fawns invisible go
With the fallow doe;
And the winds blow
Fast as the stars are slow.

Stealthily the dark haunts round
And, when the lamp goes, without sound
At a swifter bound
Than the swiftest hound,
Arrives, and all else is drowned;

And star and I and wind and deer,
Are in the dark together, – near,
Yet far, – and fear
Drums on my ear
In that sage company drear.

How weak and little is the light,
All the universe of sight,
Love and delight,
Before the might,
If you love it not, of night.

WILFRED OWEN

Futility

Move him into the sun –
Gently its touch awoke him once,
At home, whispering of fields unsown.
Always it woke him, even in France,
Until this morning and this snow.
If anything might rouse him now
The kind old sun will know.

Think how it wakes the seeds, –
Woke, once, the clays of a cold star.
Are limbs, so dear-achieved, are sides,
Full-nerved – still warm – too hard to stir?
Was it for this the clay grew tall?
– O what made fatuous sunbeams toil
To break earth's sleep at all?

Anthem for Doomed Youth

What passing-bells for these who die as cattle?
    Only the monstrous anger of the guns.
    Only the stuttering rifles' rapid rattle
Can patter out their hasty orisons.
No mockeries for them from prayers or bells,
    Nor any voice of mourning save the choirs, –
The shrill, demented choirs of wailing shells;
    And bugles calling for them from sad shires.

What candles may be held to speed them all?
    Not in the hands of boys, but in their eyes
Shall shine the holy glimmers of good-byes.
    The pallor of girls' brows shall be their pall;
Their flowers the tenderness of silent minds,
And each slow dusk a drawing-down of blinds.

Strange Meeting

It seemed that out of battle I escaped
Down some profound dull tunnel, long since scooped
Through granites which titanic wars had groined.
Yet also there encumbered sleepers groaned,
Too fast in thought or death to be bestirred.
Then, as I probed them, one sprang up, and stared
With piteous recognition in fixed eyes,
Lifting distressful hands as if to bless.
And by his smile, I knew that sullen hall,
By his dead smile I knew we stood in Hell.
With a thousand pains that vision's face was grained;
Yet no blood reached there from the upper ground,
And no guns thumped, or down the flues made moan.
'Strange friend,' I said, 'here is no cause to mourn.'
'None,' said the other, 'save the undone years,
The hopelessness. Whatever hope is yours,
Was my life also; I went hunting wild
After the wildest beauty in the world,
Which lies not calm in eyes, or braided hair,
But mocks the steady running of the hour,
And if it grieves, grieves richlier than here.
For by my glee might many men have laughed,
And of my weeping something had been left,
Which must die now. I mean the truth untold,
The pity of war, the pity war distilled.
Now men will go content with what we spoiled.
Or, discontent, boil bloody, and be spilled.
They will be swift with swiftness of the tigress,
None will break ranks, though nations trek from progress.
Courage was mine, and I had mystery,
Wisdom was mine, and I had mastery;
To miss the march of this retreating world
Into vain citadels that are not walled.
Then, when much blood had clogged their chariot-wheels
I would go up and wash them from sweet wells,
Even with truths that lie too deep for taint.
I would have poured my spirit without stint
But not through wounds; not on the cess of war.
Foreheads of men have bled where no wounds were.
I am the enemy you killed, my friend.

I knew you in this dark; for so you frowned
Yesterday through me as you jabbed and killed.
I parried; but my hands were loath and cold.
Let us sleep now....'

INDEX OF AUTHORS

INDEX OF FIRST LINES